Basic Counselling Skills for Teachers

Basic Counselling Skills for Teachers provides teachers and school staff with an accessible guide, and easy-to-apply skills, to providing counselling to students in a school setting. It looks at what counselling is and what it is not, how to recognise that a student may need counselling, creating the right environment and maintaining confidentiality.

Throughout the book, Tim Dansie provides case studies and strategies for teachers that will help them to encourage students to open up and talk whilst having a model to follow outlining a Solution-Focused Counselling approach. It includes easy-to-understand chapters on counselling for:

- grief
- bullying
- anger
- anxiety
- depression
- friendships
- career guidance
- technology addiction.

Concise and practical, this book is essential reading for teachers who want to develop their counselling skills and be able to confidently support students in many of the challenges they face on their journey through school.

Tim Dansie is a Registered Psychologist and Teacher who works in Private Practice in Adelaide, South Australia, whilst also presenting training seminars to schools throughout Australia.

Basic Counselling Skills for Teachers

Tim Dansie

LONDON AND NEW YORK

First published 2019
by Routledge
2 Park Square, Milton Park, Abingdon, Oxon OX14 4RN

and by Routledge
52 Vanderbilt Avenue, New York, NY 10017

Routledge is an imprint of the Taylor & Francis Group, an informa business

© 2019 Tim Dansie

The right of Tim Dansie to be identified as author of this work has been asserted by him in accordance with sections 77 and 78 of the Copyright, Designs and Patents Act 1988.

All rights reserved. No part of this book may be reprinted or reproduced or utilised in any form or by any electronic, mechanical, or other means, now known or hereafter invented, including photocopying and recording, or in any information storage or retrieval system, without permission in writing from the publishers.

Trademark notice: Product or corporate names may be trademarks or registered trademarks, and are used only for identification and explanation without intent to infringe.

British Library Cataloguing-in-Publication Data
A catalogue record for this book is available from the British Library

Library of Congress Cataloging-in-Publication Data
Names: Dansie, Tim, author.
Title: Basic counselling skills for teachers / Tim Dansie.
Description: Abingdon, Oxon ; New York, NY : Routledge, 2018. | Includes bibliographical references.
Identifiers: LCCN 2018044634| ISBN 9781138305595 (hardback) | ISBN 9781138305601 (pbk.) | ISBN 9780203728895 (ebook)
Subjects: LCSH: Teacher participation in educational counseling. | Teacher-student relationships.
Classification: LCC LB1027.5 .D274 2018 | DDC 371.4—dc23
LC record available at https://lccn.loc.gov/2018044634

ISBN: 978-1-138-30559-5 (hbk)
ISBN: 978-1-138-30560-1 (pbk)
ISBN: 978-0-203-72889-5 (ebk)

Typeset in Bembo
by Swales & Willis Ltd, Exeter, Devon, UK

Contents

List of figures vi
Introduction vii

1. Why are teachers good counsellors?   1
2. Why we teach problem-solving skills   4
3. Counselling for teachers   6
4. The Solution-Focused Counselling Model   35
5. Counselling techniques   47
6. Counselling for grief   52
7. Counselling to develop friendships   65
8. Counselling for career guidance   69
9. Counselling students who are developing an addiction to technology   73
10. Counselling for bullying   76
11. Counselling for anger   83
12. Counselling for anxiety   86
13. Counselling for depression   94
14. Looking after yourself when counselling   99

Appendix 101
References 107
Index 108

Figures

1	Example of working on a whiteboard	24
2	An example of a welcoming office	30
3	A good example of an office that has lots of interesting things in it	30
4	Solution-Focused Counselling Model	37
5	Model for grief counselling	59
6	The friendship circle	66
7	An example career cake	71
8	Reacting to bullying behaviours using a seesaw model	81
9	Anxiety thought blocking process	89
10	Anxiety level/Worry scale	90
11	Genogram symbols to use with students	101
12	Example of a genogram	102
13	*How are you feeling today?* model	103

Introduction

Hello and welcome to the book *Basic Counselling Skills for Teachers*. My name is Tim Dansie and I am a Registered Psychologist and Registered Teacher and at the time of writing this book, I have spent 29 years working in schools as a teacher (12 years) and psychologist (17 years). In my 17 years of private practice as a psychologist I have predominantly worked in schools helping teachers to identify and support students who have behavioural or learning needs. Along the way I have conducted and still continue to hold many training days for staff of schools across a wide range of areas; this book is based on the seminar of the same name which I have been running in schools for 15 years.

In my years working as a psychologist, predominantly with students, I have learnt that one of the best ways to achieve good outcomes for students is to have a combined counselling approach with me, the psychologist, and with a teacher or teachers at school. The reason for this is that I may see a student on a weekly, monthly or fortnightly basis whereas a teacher has access to students every day of the week. The teachers can then reinforce the skills that are being worked on every day whilst also addressing any concerns that can present on a daily basis. This combined approach is very effective and the reason why I encourage all teachers to develop basic counselling skills.

Throughout the book I have included case studies, though I have changed the names of the clients for confidentiality reasons. I have also included the answers to questions I pose to teachers who are working day-to-day in a counselling setting in regard to topics such as working with students who are experiencing grief and students who have difficulty in forming friendships. A lot of the information in the book has been provided to me by the many wonderful teachers who have attended my seminar. Please enjoy *Basic Counselling Skills for Teachers*.

In today's ever-changing society it has become increasingly clear that our teachers are being asked to fulfil so many more roles for children, as well as teaching. One of these roles is the job of counsellor. This book will help teachers gain an understanding of the counselling process but it also covers how to teach students to learn to solve many of their own day-to-day challenges that are all a part of learning and growing up.

Basic Counselling Skills for Teachers looks at what counselling is and what it is not, how to recognise that a student may need counselling, how to help students develop and maintain friendships, and maintaining confidentiality; it also introduces the Solution-Focused Counselling Model that can be easily learnt and applied to counselling situations. In the second part of the book topics such as counselling for grief, depression, anxiety, technology use, bullying and anger are discussed, with ideas provided on how to work with students who are experiencing challenges from within these areas.

We must never forget that the role of teachers is primarily to teach and to know how and who to refer to for counselling for students. However, in some circumstances it is the teacher who will be the primary source of counselling for a student because the student has identified them as the person of trust and the person they have a good relationship with. This is why it is very important for all teachers to have some basic counselling skills.

Case study – why all school staff need some counselling skills

A school groundsman approached me whilst I was working as a middle school counsellor, very concerned about a 14-year-old boy who attended the school. The groundsman explained to me that the boy had starting hanging around him at recess and lunchtime asking lots of questions about what it was he did at school. Over time the boy started telling the groundsman about what was happening in his life, leading to the concern and subsequent approach to me.

The groundsman explained that the boy had spoken about a domestic violence situation at his home which had happened recently and how the boy was scared. What was worrying the groundsman was that he did not know what to say to the boy or how to help him. As a result I worked with the groundsman and gave him some ideas on how he could get the boy to come in and talk to me. The groundsman was taught to slowly introduce the idea of working with the school counsellor. To his credit the groundsman said to the boy "When I am confused or not sure about things I often have a chat to the school counsellor. He is a really friendly and helpful person and I am happy to go with you if you want." Fortunately the plan worked; the boy came to my office with the groundsman and we all talked together.

One of the most important points to come from our conversation was the answer the boy gave when he was asked why he spoke to the groundsman. The response was very simple: "The groundsman was kind and he listened to me." What became apparent was the boy did not have close friends at school and he was somewhat of a loner. Over time, the groundsman and I helped the boy through a number of challenges throughout his education.

The point is, all people in schools need to have some counselling skills; if a student chooses you to talk to, you need to know how to help. Some basic counselling skills are useful for all.

I hope this book provides you some skills, strategies and processes you can follow when you need to provide counselling skills to help one of your students.

1 Why are teachers good counsellors?

This is a very good question. What I have observed over my years working in schools is that teachers and school staff make very good counsellors due to having a number of very good innate skills. Some of the skills I have observed are:

- **Being very well organised.** The day-to-day running of a classroom requires great organisation skills. Teachers will plan and teach lessons, mark work, communicate with fellow staff, parents and students, work on extra curricular activities and complete ongoing staff professional development (I am sure there are things I have missed). To do all of these things you need to be well organised, which teachers are.

A good counsellor is well organised because they manage their time well, plan counselling sessions, communicate well with clients (in children's cases, often parents), complete ongoing professional development and genuinely care about people. The similarities in teachers and counsellors are there in the micro and macro skills.

- **Having the ability to think very quickly whilst on the go.** When you spend some time in a classroom watching a teacher, count the number of decisions that are made in a five-minute period across a wide range of areas. The numbers are huge. As a result of this, teachers develop the ability to think fast and make decisions on the spot. It is this ability to think on their feet that I see as a vital skill in counselling.

When counselling, more often than not you are not going to know what will be said. A counsellor who is rigid in their counselling style may not suit many clients – particularly students – whereas a counsellor who can think fast is likely to be able to adapt their method to meet the need of the client.

Good counsellors think quickly and make decisions on the approach that best suits a client. Teachers have to do this all day and have the ability to adapt and be flexible: a key component to good counselling.

- **Good problem-solving skills.** Teachers are constantly solving problems in a classroom on a day-to-day basis. The role of a teacher has changed so much over the last 20 years due to societal changes; this has led to teachers needing much greater problem-solving skills. When watching teachers it is easy to see this in action. Issues in junior primary such as not having a drink bottle, forgetting lunch, losing a book, not having a pencil, losing a hat, etc., happen every day. Teachers solve these issues quickly and efficiently.

As students get older the problems become more complex but fortunately teachers have the skills and, in most cases, the support networks to cope. Counsellors also work with clients in teaching them problem-solving skills. The only difference is teachers tend to solve the problems due to it being too busy in the classroom, whereas counsellors will work with clients so they learn to solve the problems themselves. An easy adjustment for teachers, provided time permits.

- **Good skills in teaching strategies to students that help them.** Teachers teach and in doing so develop a wide range of techniques to convey information and impart skills to students. So much of counselling is in the ability to teach skills to clients that can be applied to the situation when needed. Teachers know how students learn and how to pass on information in a variety of methods.
- **Good role modelling behaviours.** Teachers have the opportunity to role model so many behaviours and in doing so they can teach students great coping skills. By using examples from day-to-day life, teachers can show students how they cope with a variety of situations.

Case study – role modelling

A Year 7 teacher walks into the classroom first thing in the morning and writes the following on the board – "Please sit quietly and read for ten minutes as I have had the worst morning possible." The students appear somewhat shocked, but they comply. After ten minutes, the teacher gets up, takes three deep breaths and says, "Thank you for being quiet. I have had the worst morning. On my way to school I was nearly in a car accident and it has really shaken me up. Sitting quietly has allowed me to take some deep breaths, reassure myself that I am okay and settle myself down for the day."

What have the students learnt through this? They learn that teachers have bad moments in a day but they have strategies to cope. The students also learn that when things go wrong, sitting quietly and taking some deep breaths is a strategy that can be used to become calm.

Counsellors will also role model strategies; however, teachers get so many more opportunities as they spend such large amounts of time with students. The use of art, drama, writing, physical activity and music can be helpful in getting a student to talk and as teachers have skills in these areas, counselling for teachers can be much easier.

- **A good sense of humour, which goes a long way in counselling students.** Many students would question whether their maths teacher, who is always very stern, has a good sense of humour. However, having spent a lot of time over the years with teachers I can honestly say that most of them do have a good sense of humour and they can make students laugh and smile. I think one of the essences of being a good counsellor is to be able to make a client smile despite how devastating a situation may be.

Teachers read situations well and they are able to use humour to help students see the funny side of things – that can lead to gaining perspective. A sense of humour can never be discounted in counselling and teachers do it well.

- **Teachers and school staff were once students themselves so they understand what it is like to be at school.** All teachers went through school. They understand what it is like to be a student but also how the world has changed. Being able to reflect on experiences and use that experience to help current students is invaluable. Life experience helps and teachers, having seen many students over the years, are in a good position to read a student through their behaviour and then guide them through the school journey. You can't buy experience.
- **Teachers have the ability and opportunity to build relationships with students.** Through their jobs teachers have the opportunity to work with students every day. In my practice as a psychologist, this very rarely happens and more often than not it is due to a person being in a hospital setting – but even upon release, appointments tend to be weekly. As a result of daily interactions, teachers can work with a student to build quality counselling relationships quickly.

When working with students who have anxiety, daily interactions can be a huge advantage as the teacher can receive regular feedback and work with a student to implement little changes that are working towards an agreed goal. Teachers can also be there to correct with kindness when things go wrong, provide positive reinforcement to good behaviour changes and act as a mediator to help a student communicate with other teachers, parents and peers.

It seems logical that when so many of a student's challenges are based around school, why not have people at school who can work with the student to help them work their way through the challenges.

Finally, and most importantly, teachers and school staff care about students and it is the caring and genuine concern of a student's well-being that leads to teachers and school staff doing the little extra things that mean so much to a student in need.

Teachers make excellent counsellors and the previous indicators are a small snapshot of how they can use their teaching skills to help students.

Having conducted counselling skills seminars over the last ten years I am always astounded by not only how quickly the teachers learn counselling skills, but also the passion they have for counselling and helping students.

2 Why we teach problem-solving skills

A big part of counselling in schools is the teaching of problem-solving skills; in this book I will provide a very straightforward and structured model for problem-solving skills counselling. However, I think it is relevant to all students, as a part of their mental health education, for teachers and school staff to teach problem-solving skills. Here are the reasons why.

1. To prepare students for life after school.

    Often I am asked to define what a successful education of a student is. My answer is, "a successful education is one where a student leaves school and is able to enter into a vocation of interest within their capabilities". At present I am seeing students who are not at all prepared for life after school due to not having the skills to cope outside a structured, routine-based environment. A big part of this is that students do not know how to solve problems: due to never having the need, but also because they have not been taught how to.

    It is evident in society today that we are seeing increased numbers of young people being diagnosed with mental health conditions; I believe some of this can be attributed to students not having the skills to cope or problem-solve outside of a school environment. By teaching a problem-solving model we can equip students for some of the challenges that they will face in life after school. A study commissioned by Mission Australia in conjunction with the Black Dog Institute in 2016 found that, of the students surveyed, one in four aged 15 to 19 years old met the criteria for having a probable serious mental illness. The top three causes were stress, school/study or depression.

2. To build resilience.

    The teaching of problem-solving skills directly helps students to build resilience for when things go wrong. In my practice I am meeting more and more students who simply do not have any: this is because they don't know what to do when their day-to-day expectations of life are not met. A structured problem-solving model provides students with a process to follow, so when an event occurs they have the skills to be able to stop, think and then work through a process to solve the problem.

    Teachers can also ask a student to work through the model before coming to them for further help if required. We must remember there will always be events where direct teacher help is needed but often students can work things out for themselves. The question I encourage teachers to always ask is "How can I help you?" This is the response to a problem question rather than giving the student the answer directly.

3   To deal with helicopter parents.

    In today's society we are seeing more and more parents who completely control their children's lives. Some of the terms used to describe these parents are *helicopter parents* (hovers over a child to make sure everything is okay), *lawn mower parents* (clear the pathway for their child), *gunship parent* (more extreme version of the helicopter parent). The end outcome is this style of parenting produces children who have no problem-solving skills at all, because they have never had to solve a problem. By teaching a problem-solving skills model and providing the opportunity to use it, students learn to solve problems for themselves. The challenge is to ask the helicopter parents to stay grounded.

4   To create enthusiasm for learning.

    Learning how to solve problems can create an enthusiasm for learning for students, due to them knowing how to work through challenges and having the skills to tackle problems that are presented as a part of learning. Often students who are disengaged with learning can be engaged by providing them with hands on problem-solving tasks. Part of the learning for students is how to solve the problem in a structured manner.

The teaching of problem-solving is a part of counselling in schools but it is also a very good day-to-day life skill to teach all students. It assists in developing adults who have the ability to work through issues as they arise and creates solutions to help them cope. I see the building of resilience as an important component of a child's development given the challenges students are now facing as they progress through school and into adulthood. Resilience can be created by learning to solve problems.

The Mission Australia study in 2016 indicated that 25% of adolescent students will experience some form of mental illness whilst attending school. The teaching of problem-solving skills will help to reduce this figure.

3 Counselling for teachers

Whenever I run the *Basic Counselling Skills for Teachers* seminar I always ask the group two questions at the start. The first is, "What is counselling?"; the second is "What is not counselling?" When I ask what counselling is I ask participants to focus on the behaviours of counselling, taking into account how we present ourselves, the environment and communication required to counsel effectively.

What is counselling?

Here are some of the most common responses.

Talking to students

Taking the time to sit and talk whilst also showing an interest in a student. Learning about what the student's interests are, what school is like for them, who their friends are, etc.

Solving problems

Working with students to solve problems. This is not solving the problem for a student but working with a student to teach them the steps in solving the problems they are experiencing.

Mediating disputes

Working with two or more people to assist in solving conflicts.

Listening

Simply sitting and listening. Using active listening skills shows a student that you are really with them and you care.

> ### Case study – active listening
>
> When working as a school counsellor I had a 16-year-old girl come in who was quite visibly distressed. I sat and I listened, nodding, making body gestures to show I was listening, used words such as "really", "tell me more", "wow", "okay", "my goodness", etc. to show I was listening.
>
> After 45 minutes the girl stood up and said "Thank you Mr Dansie, I feel so much better now." All I had done was sit and listen and show an active concern for the girl's well-being.

Caring

Doing the little things like saying hello in the school yard, following up on agreements and ensuring the student knows you are there for them.

Being there

Making time for students. A good counsellor knows time boundaries yet has the uncanny ability to be able to make time for students. This can be done through arriving early to school, giving up a recess or lunchtime or staying after school. Even when there is not a free time during the day, a student knows that the teacher is there for them. In some cases just having this knowledge makes a huge difference for a student.

Providing a safe place to talk

A key ingredient to counselling is providing students with a safe place to talk, but also a place that makes a student feel welcome.

Showing empathy

Talking to students and through language and body language letting the student know you are trying to understand how they are feeling at the time. To me, empathy is trying to gain an understanding of what it is like to be in the shoes of the client. No person can truly fully understand what it must be like; however, making the effort to understand how a person is feeling and how their thoughts influence their behaviours is demonstrating empathy. Good counsellors have the ability to show empathy through the language they use and the body language displayed.

We must also remember to be very careful with empathy. I once met a counsellor who explained how they were working with a young student whose dog had died. The counsellor said to the student "I know how you feel", to which the student replied "No you don't, it wasn't your dog that died." The student was correct. The point is, the language of empathy must be carefully used.

Body language

Good counsellors can convey so much to a client through body language. A counsellor who presents as over zealous can scare a student whilst a counsellor who is too relaxed can convey a message of not being interested. I do not get too worked up about body language, with my main rule being do not cross your arms. The crossing of arms gives a very negative message. I also remind counsellors to be mindful of eye contact as some students can find too much eye contact very off-putting. Be yourself, whilst bearing these points in mind.

Case study – body language

A good way to remember body language is through the Egan **SOLER** acronym. In 1986 Gerard Egan created the acronym SOLER as a guide for counsellors to help them to remember to use positive body language.

(continued)

(continued)

SOLER stands for:

S – squarely

The first important part of communication is how you posture yourself in relationship to the other party. With your face facing theirs, it shows that you are engaging, interested and actively listening. You can have your shoulders turned a little away to dispel any feelings of intimidation, but your face should be square onto the other person – hence the term 'squarely'.

O – open

This openness refers again to posturing. Ensuring that arms and legs are not crossed will convey a sense of ease to the other person. As above, this openness in body posture will stop feelings of intimidation from occurring.

L – lean

By leaning towards the other person, a sense of care and genuine interest will be conveyed to the other party. Simply leaning forward will automatically make the other person feel that their concerns are being heard and understood and this will instil further ease and facilitate openness.

E – eye contact

Eye contact is an important part of showing we are listening to a person; however, we must be conscious of not staring. Looking a person in the eye whilst nodding and using verbal responses such as "yes", "okay", "go on" shows a person we are truly with them.

R – relax

This is an obvious, but sometimes forgotten, aspect. One must relax before communicating with the person sat before them. If you are fidgeting or showing any anxiety, it will be conveyed to the other person. They will then think you are not interested in them, or they will take on your tension.

Students pick up very quickly on body language so it is important to get it right – as is making a student feel very welcome in a counselling setting.

Prompting

Counselling is about having the tricks to prompt a client into talking. Charts, questionnaires, games and questions are all important tools to use when prompting a reluctant client to talk. One of my favourite prompts (and one that is hard to learn how to use) is silence. When we are silent, often the client will talk to break the silence. Good counsellors use silence effectively as a counselling tool.

Allowing a person to tell their story

Counsellors have the ability to make a client feel comfortable and free to talk and tell their story without interrupting or diverting onto another topic. Knowing when to use phrases such as "Tell me more" or "What happened next?", combined with body language, allows a person to open up and tell their story.

Being free of judgement

Counsellors are free of judgement; clients are not judged on their actions or behaviours. The client is the most important person and counselling is about helping them without judging them.

Keeping confidentiality

A key to all counselling is trust. We can't hide from the fact that this is very difficult at times and confidentiality must be broken. This will be addressed in a later chapter; however, trust is critical in any counselling relationship and confidentiality goes a long way to creating trust.

Representing students

Often in a counselling role, teachers and staff will represent students and have discussions with parents, teachers and allied health professionals on their behalf.

Case study – advocating for students

A 13-year-old student presents to me for counselling. In our discussions the student explained that she was finding keeping up with the workload exceptionally challenging and that the move from a primary school setting where she had predominantly one teacher, to a middle school setting where she had a number of teachers, was overwhelming. The student was very upset because of her perceptions of the expectations of her parents and also due to the lack of control being experienced in relation to her studies.

To support the student, I first gained permission to talk to her parents and teachers as a starting point. I then met with the student's parents and teachers to explain how she was feeling – but more importantly to work towards strategies to help.

Sometimes students are scared to speak up and ask for help so as counsellors we can support and advocate on their behalf.

Teaching of skills

The teaching of skills is a big part of counselling. Students will often need to learn new skills so they can apply the skills-based strategy to a situation. Skills in how to control anger, identify the signs of anxiety, respond to stress, speak up in front of a group are all some of the typical skills that students often need help to develop. A part of counselling is taking the time to develop the skills students need in order to be confident within the school (and sometimes home) environment.

Having tools to help students talk and the availability to do so

Teachers can access a wide variety of tools to help students open up and talk. There is a good range of prompts, puzzles, posters and games which will help students to relax. Furthermore, the greatest advantage teachers have is that they can talk to a student on every school day if required. This allows the setting of short-term goals, which can then be monitored, adapted and implemented on a daily basis as needed.

Having worked in counselling I think I have some good skills in getting students to open up and talk about what is happening in their life. However, sometimes even the best skills in the world will not help.

Case study – when a student will not talk

I once had a Year 9 student named Catherine sent to my office. Catherine was angry and she sat with a scowl on her face. I was friendly, asking usual get-to-know-you questions, to which I got nothing. Catherine had decided that she was not going to talk. Thinking quickly, I went to the video of the movie *Good Will Hunting* – the psychologist and client counselling scene where the two just sat and looked at each other for an hour.

Catherine smirked at this and I said "Catherine I understand that you are angry and that you don't want to talk. That is okay but I want you to know that if you ever do want to talk I am here and happy to listen." Catherine walked out.

Five years later I bumped into Catherine in a shop. "Mr Dansie, do you remember me?" Catherine asked. "How could I forget you, Catherine?" was my response. Catherine said "Do you remember the time I was in your office?" "Of course," I said. She continued "I was that close to talking to you but the best thing was, once I had calmed down, I knew you cared and that made me feel so much better."

What did I learn? I learnt that you can still make a difference by being there and even the best tools in the world will not make a student talk if they don't want to. The challenge for teachers and school staff is to identify a wide range of ways to help students open up and talk. The Appendix at the end of the book contains some ideas that help.

Knowing referral sources

A very important part of counselling is knowing your referral sources. Who can help you? In today's world we are very lucky to have so many online resources, support agencies and a greater understanding of the issues which impact upon our students. Having a list of resources is a very big part of counselling in schools as it allows staff to direct students to the best possible support available.

When I am asked "What is counselling?" I believe it encompasses all of the above at different points of time; however, I run with this definition: counselling is the functioning relationship between a counsellor and a client in which the counsellor is working to assist the client to understand their thoughts and behaviours and how they impact upon oneself, whilst developing strategies to improve day-to-day thinking and behaviours. A simple definition of counselling is: taking the time to get to know and help someone to make positive changes in their life.

What is not counselling?

Unfortunately, many students and adults are put off of any counselling due to having bad experiences at schools. This then can lead to a reluctance to seek any support in the future when stress or uncertainty present, leading to a significant decline in overall wellbeing and then a big crash. It is so important that students have a positive attitude towards counselling and that counselling is perceived as a good process to the individual.

Sometimes, due to lack of training, empathy or the ability to build a rapport with a student, counselling is done poorly. Having counselled a lot of students over the last 15 years and spent a lot of time in schools listening to teachers, I have learnt what *not to do* when counselling students.

The following are examples of what counselling is *not*.

Telling people what to do

The temptation when counselling is to simply tell a student what to do to solve the presenting issue. This saves time and can sometimes provide a short-term solution; however, there are a number of problems associated with doing this. Firstly, the student does not learn to work through and solve problems for themselves – this skill is not learnt for future reference. Simply just telling someone what to do can create a learned helplessness situation where a student always becomes reliant on someone solving things for them.

Secondly, without having taken the time to get to know a student, a counsellor may not be aware as to whether the student has the skills to follow the instructions. Counselling is about getting to know the student and their capacity to learn and implement new skills. Telling a student what to do when they don't have the skills to fulfil the instructions is setting up the student for failure.

Thirdly, telling a student what to do is based around the values and ideals of the counsellor and not necessarily the student. This can lead to a student questioning the advice as it goes against their beliefs and they will not be able to envisage the consequences.

Finally, good counselling is based around a positive relationship of communication where a position of power does not exist. By telling someone what to do, a position of power is assumed by the counsellor. In schools this is tricky as it is expected that students do what teachers and staff say, but in counselling the best outcomes are achieved by working together on an equal level.

Counselling is not telling a person what to do.

Not listening to the whole story

Often in the busyness of a school day a teacher or staff member does not have the time to sit and listen to get the whole story from a student. As a result of this a student can feel cut off and not heard, resulting in the student being reluctant to go back to talk further.

Not getting the whole story can also lead to the primary issue not being discussed by the student. Comments such as "We only really scratched the surface" or "I didn't really get to say what was really troubling me as the counsellor just went with the first thing I raised" are not uncommon when working with students.

Rushing or not taking time to listen to the whole story is not counselling.

Having bias

On occasion, teachers and counsellors can have a bias based on their own personal experiences or perceptions of a student. This can lead to students feeling that the counsellor is biased against them or towards others. Good counsellors are value-free and do not have a bias. Learning to be value-free at all times is an important skill in counselling.

Holding grudges

Holding grudges can occur particularly in circumstances such as bullying. Having knowledge of how a student has behaved towards others can certainly influence a counsellor's interactions when working with the student who has caused distress for other students. Counselling is not holding grudges or using prior knowledge to influence attitudes towards a student. It is treating every student as an equal and every situation on face value without bias.

Not listening – being distracted

As already mentioned, listening is critical to any counselling relationship; too often, teachers and counsellors don't actively listen and only hear what they want to hear. This can be very frustrating for the student, who leaves the session feeling as though they have not been heard and questioning the point of talking to a counsellor.

Another disappointing factor in counselling is when the counsellor is constantly distracted. This can be by noise, movement outside of the room, people knocking on the door or walking in, mobile phones and computers. I understand it is not always possible to have a perfectly quiet room but there are no excuses for looking at or answering a mobile phone. Minimise distractions and put the phone on do not disturb. I always ask counsellors to consider how clients are perceiving them during a counselling session. Does the client see you as engaged or just not with them? Not listening and being distracted are common mistakes made by counsellors.

Placing your own values first

Too often counsellors take their own values and ideals into a counselling session with students. The difficulty in this is that a student's values may be completely different to those of a counsellor and this can lead to very confused students. Counselling is not imparting your own ideals onto a student; rather it is listening and working with the student to support them to improve their overall well-being.

Confusing discipline with counselling

In some circumstances a teacher will need to be both a counsellor and also the person who enforces discipline where needed. In a perfect world the two would never be confused and different staff members would fill each of the roles. However, what must be clarified is that counselling is not enforcing negative consequences on a person due to them making a poor behavioural choice. That is a punishment and is part of the discipline process completed by school staff.

Unfortunately, sometimes the two get confused. It is possible to fulfil both roles, but in order to be successful good relationships must be had between the staff member and the student – the staff member should also clarify in what capacity they are acting when talking to the student. For example, a staff member could say "In my role as a teacher I must work with you and look at a consequence for your behaviour." What I have found is that when the staff member works with the student to establish a consequence, the change in behaviour is likely to occur much faster compared to when a consequence is given without any discussion.

Breaking confidentiality

Confidentiality is critical to any counselling relationship as it builds trust. Breaking confidentiality must occur at times, but staff must not disclose private information about a student unless mandated to do so. I have heard of situations where staff have disclosed information inappropriately to other students, causing more distress for the student seeking help. This often happens when counselling for bullying and the victim receives more bullying for speaking up.

Not taking the issue seriously

All students need to feel listened to and their issues treated with respect and concern. Counselling is not dismissing an issue as being minor or not worthy of time. To the student it is important and thus the student needs to feel listened to and supported. On occasion, staff members will dismiss an issue by saying something like "It is just a phase they are going through" or "It is just an adolescent thing." This does not help the student.

Giving advice

The temptation in counselling is to give advice; it is quick and it certainly can help. Unfortunately, this does not teach students strategies or processes to learn to solve the challenge they currently face nor the ones they will face in the future. Giving advice can also lead to bias based on the counsellor's view of a person or situation.

Poor body language

This goes without saying too much. Students pick up on poor body language and will react according to what they see. This can lead to students not talking and being resistant to further counselling.

Showing sympathy not empathy

I always ask "What is the difference between sympathy and empathy?" The answer to me is in the language that is used. When being sympathetic the language is along the lines of "You poor thing" or "That is so sad", whereas empathy is "That sounds like a sad situation to me" or "It sounds like you are very upset." The language we use and our body language will determine if we are being sympathetic or empathetic. There is a time for sympathy but empathy is critical for counselling.

Confusing counselling with behavioural management

In some cases, students are forced into a counselling situation as a result of their behaviour because parents and teachers have the belief that counselling is the solution to the behaviour, without examining its cause. This is particularly unsuccessful when the student is angry. In many school cases behaviour management strategies instigated by the teacher or behaviour management coordinator within the school are the appropriate action, rather than counselling.

Forcing a student into counselling

Forcing a student to attend counselling against their will does not work as the student is not likely to engage. For counselling to succeed the student needs to buy in to the process and understand the reason as to why counselling is needed.

Unfortunately, many students have a poor perception of what counselling is due to having a negative experience in the counselling process; often the primary causes are many of the above items listed above. Counselling is many things across a wide variety of settings, but the fundamental components are building a relationship with the client, listening and then supporting the client to make positive changes in their life.

Allowing your own personal baggage to get in the way

Before we begin any counselling, we need to understand and identify whether there is anything personal that could influence how effective we are going to be in a counselling situation. When I first started counselling I vividly remember having great difficulty in working with students, or parents of students, on situations relating to cancer. This was because my mother fought a long battle with cancer and when I was counselling I would stop listening and I would start thinking of my own personal experience. My personal baggage was inhibiting my counselling. What did I do?

I learnt a very important skill which I strongly encourage all counsellors to gain – and that is to ask for help. The client is always the priority and I want all of my clients to have the best possible help; if that means I am not the best person to help them, I need to find whoever that person is. I asked our school chaplain to work with the student and I sat in on the sessions. Over time I learnt to suppress my own feelings and become an effective counsellor, but I still believe the best lesson for me was that I learnt my strengths and limitations. When working today I always refer on to people who I believe are the best to help if my own personal baggage gets in the way of counselling or I am not the best person.

When it comes to personal baggage some types that present are listed here.

- **Separation** – a counsellor who has had a breakdown of a relationship can have their own experience influence their counselling.
- **Grief** – our own experiences of grief can surface and influence how well we listen.
- **Bullying** – a counsellor who has experienced this themselves may take a different approach when working with the bully.
- **Own school experiences** – a counsellor who experienced difficulty at school may focus more on their own experiences rather than listening to the client.
- **Experiences of own children at school** – a counsellor can reflect on what their own children went through at school rather than listening to the experiences of the student before them.
- **Parental pressure** – a counsellor may feel pressure from the parents of the student and this is apparent in the interaction with a student.

Life experience is very important in counselling and we can use our own personal experiences to guide us. However, if our own personal baggage stops us from really listening and clouds our work, the best thing to do is to be honest with the client and find someone who will best to help the student whilst we work on building our own skills. Never be scared to ask for help in counselling and always look to provide the best possible support for a student.

Knowing your strengths and weaknesses

Whilst we are on personal baggage, I think it is important to know our own strengths and weaknesses. In practice I am very clear to clients about the work I am prepared to do and the work that is not my area of expertise. For example, I will always refer clients with an eating disorder to a person who specialises in this field. I will always refer clients who are self-harming to a person who specialises in this area.

Case study – personal baggage

From a personal perspective, when I first started working as a psychologist at a school I found it very difficult to work with any client who was talking about cancer. This was due to my mother having a long battle (six years) with cancer which resulted in her passing away. I found I would stop listening effectively as my own feelings and memories would come flooding back to me. What I learnt was to refer on to another counsellor at school and I would sit in on the sessions. Over time I learnt to control my own feelings but the best thing I did was to recognise my weakness and guide the student to the person who could provide the best support.

Within schools this is not always possible; however, we need to know our areas of strength and areas of weakness. Where possible always refer on if the needs of a student are in an area where you don't feel comfortable. Sometimes this can mean going to an appointment with a student to support them whilst they meet a new counsellor. What is important is letting the student know that you are there, but that you want the best possible support for them and this is the process.

Case study – knowing yourself as a counsellor

I am acutely aware of my own weaknesses when counselling and I am always working towards improvement. When first starting counselling in a school I had to work very hard at being empathetic. This was highlighted when I had a student called Kimberly enter my office one day – to my surprise Kimberly entered by herself (Kimberly normally had three or four personal assistants who accompanied her throughout the day).

Kimberly was a very powerful 14-year-old who exerted her power and influence over many students at school and socially away from school. In my role of counsellor, I had seen many students who Kimberly had upset in some way and here was Kimberly herself looking upset. Kimberly sat down and burst into tears saying how her boyfriend had broken off the relationship. Many tears were flowing. This was a time where I had to really practise empathy as I knew how many students Kimberly had upset in the past through her behaviour and attitude towards others.

Kimberly was okay and I used the situation to help her become aware of her behaviour, resulting in a much nicer and friendlier Kimberly. I always remember that I must practise empathy; there will be times when your students will need support even though their behaviour has sometimes caused problems for many.

"A glass of empathy for breakfast every morning" is what I encourage for anyone working with students in a school or counselling setting. This means doing their best to try and understand how a student is feeling and recognising the impact that their feelings are having on their day-to-day ability to function. We must also work towards knowing our strengths whilst improving our weaknesses. We must learn as counsellors to not judge our clients – empathy is a skill I constantly practise.

It all starts with listening

Of all the skills of counselling, listening is the most important. We really need to convey to our students that we are listening and with them. The most important type of listening is *active listening* – this is showing through our body language and verbal responses that we are listening well and taking in the information.

I learnt from this experience that sometimes all we need to do is to be there and listen. Often in counselling the client will solve things and get clarity just through talking. The role of the counsellor is to listen and give the client the opportunity to talk.

So how do we develop our active listening skills?

The following are active listening skills to develop:

Allow your body language to reflect your response. If you respond with "Wow" show that on your face. If you respond with "How did that happen?" show curiosity on your face. Let your facial expressions reflect your listening.

Use lots of verbal responses such as "Yes", "Okay", "Wow", whilst also nodding, leaning forward or back depending on the response and prompts such as "Tell me more" or "What happened next?"

Seek clarity through verbal responses. Ask questions such as "Am I right in thinking that you were . . . because of . . . ?" or "It sounds to me that you were feeling very . . . because of . . . ." This provides the student with the opportunity to give us clarity.

Case study – listening and seeking clarity

I once worked with a student who I thought was upset about the breakdown of a friendship, but when I said "It sounds to me like you are feeling sad because you are no longer friends with Jack" the student responded with "No not at all, I am upset because some of the others in the group believe Jack's version of the events and not mine. I never really liked Jack but liked the group."

Through seeking clarity, I was able to be corrected by the student as I had misread his reason for being upset.

Reflecting feelings is a big part of active listening. Using statements such as "It seems to me that you are feeling angry because of . . . allows a student to confirm their feelings whilst also giving the counsellor guidance in what direction to take the counselling. A follow-up to this question may be "So out of ten, how angry are you?" Another way of reflecting feelings can be through the observation of a student's body language. A statement could be "It looks to me through your body language that you are feeling . . . because of . . . . The reflecting of feelings can help a student to understand for themselves how they are really feeling.

When reflecting feelings, I would never come out and ask a student "How do you feel?" or "How did that make you feel?" This is a personal thing for me and here is the reason.

I was introduced to a 12-year-old boy who had already been to see three counsellors in the last 12 months, with all of the outcomes being unsuccessful. Automatically I was worried given three previous counsellors had not been able to form any type of relationship with the boy. Rather than go and sit down I decided that it was best we go for a walk and have a chat whilst we were walking. Things were going well and out of the blue the boy said "Please don't ask me how I feel, everyone always asks me how I feel." What I learnt from the boy was that he did not like the idea of counselling as he saw it as stereotypical American television therapy where every second question was about how you feel, unfortunately the three previous counsellors had asked him this question, much to his displeasure. My learning was do not make counselling stereotypical, let it suit the needs of the student.

I cannot stress the importance of active listening enough. So often when working with parents my message is talk less and listen more. Too often, parents, like teachers, are so quick to jump in and solve the problems rather than taking the time to listen and then respond with "So how can I help you?"

We have two ears to listen with and only one mouth to talk with!

How do we know a student may need counselling?

More often than not students will give us clues that something is not right in their world. As teachers it is up to us to take notice, make a mental note, check with our peers to see if they have noticed something and then keep a closer eye on the student.

The following are common signs or symptoms that would suggest a student may need counselling, or at a minimum an enquiry about their well-being.

- **Absenteeism** – student is away frequently from school. A student who is constantly late or appears flustered in the morning can also be a cue for counselling.
- **Not wanting to go home** – a student who seems to be reluctant to leave the classroom; however, be thoughtful here. I have a daughter who was always late out of class because she loved her teacher so much and she wanted to stay and talk.
- **Crying** – the easiest of all the cues to recognise and one that requires instant attention.
- **Withdrawn** – a student who has gone from being friendly and talkative to quiet and distant.
- **Cues** such as eye contact and body language can tell us that a student is not happy.
- **Diagnosed conditions** such as ASD, PTSD, ADHD – often specialists will write in reports that a student should be mentored by a person at school who has day-to-day contact with the student. When working with ASD students this becomes very important in the teaching of social skills and behaviour management.
- **Behaviour change** – when we notice that the behaviour of a student has changed over a period of time. A student's behaviour can change due to fatigue, frustration or a number of adolescent reasons – but what we are looking for here is change over a period of time. "How much time?" you are thinking. I always suggest a week at a minimum. Background information on a student who is showing signs of behavioural change is critical as it may tell us the reason why the change is occurring.

Case study – student who was grieving

A teacher came to see me worried that a 14-year-old student had become very quiet, withdrawn and her academic results had started to drop off. The student was relatively new to the school but had settled in really well and was involved in a number of school-based activities. The only background information of any relevance was that the girl had moved school on a number of occasions due to her parents being employed within the armed forces.

As I did not know the girl I suggested that the teacher find a moment where she could have a quick one-on-one chat, just to ask about how things were going for the girl at school. When the moment presented after school and the chat occurred the answer became clear: that girl had been told by her parents that they were moving again due to another posting interstate and the girl was devastated. The girl explained how she just loved being at school, the students, teachers, subjects but also that she had finally made some very good friends. We now understood the cause of the behaviour.

Fortunately, this story had a very happy ending as the girl's parents and school were able to set up a very good home stay situation so the girl could stay at school whilst returning to visit her parents for school holidays. I can also say that the girl has been very successful in her studies and she is currently working in a field where she is supporting students who have learning difficulties.

- **Academic attainment dropping** – this is an area where caution is needed and more often than not, discussions with teachers, parents and the special education team are required. The challenge here is to determine whether the student needs counselling support or learning support. It can be the case that the two go hand in hand as I have worked with many students whose behaviour has deteriorated in the classroom due to finding the work expectations too hard; as a result they need some counselling to learn how to modify their behaviour within the classroom whilst also learning to ask for help.

Case study – student with learning difficulties

A student who had just transitioned from primary school into high school with a large number of friends was displaying behaviours that were disruptive within the classroom environment. Of interest was that the behaviours were only displayed in certain subjects. Discussions with parents revealed that the boy had found learning challenging in the past and that he had been well supported at his previous school with learning.

Within the new school the boy was not coping with many changes such as increased homework, moving from classroom to classroom and changes in teaching styles. Subjects such as P.E., Art, Technology and Music were fine but Maths and English were a real challenge. As a result of not coping the boy was being rude and disrupting the class. When talking with the boy he revealed that he needed help with his learning and that he felt completely overwhelmed in class. After talking to the teachers some modifications to the curriculum were made and this, combined with some counselling for the boy, led to an increase in confidence and self-esteem in regard to learning and the behaviours ceased.

- **Artwork** – a student's artwork can reveal a lot about what a student is thinking or feeling. Our younger students through drawing can provide us with a lead to ask questions about what the drawing is about. Through looking and asking we can learn a lot about what a student is feeling. Older students can convey dark thoughts through their artwork and it is important that teachers ask students questions about their work and the thinking behind it. The challenge here is to make sure that we don't influence the artwork as through art students can express themselves, which can be a part of a healing process. This is also the case when students are writing.
- **Writing** – a student's writing can reveal a lot about them, which again allows a teacher to ask questions to ensure a student is okay.

Case study – identifying a student who needs counselling through their writing

I vividly remember walking to my office after recess and seeing an English teacher rushing towards me waving papers. I knew this was not going to be good. What was presented to me was an essay by a Year 9 boy named Tim, whose essay was very expressive and brutal (words are hard to find to describe it). Fortunately, I knew Tim as I was his P.E. teacher and after a lesson I caught him so we could have a quick chat.

I asked Tim about his essay. Tim's head dropped, he paused, looked up and calmly said "Mr Dansie, I just wanted to make an impact." "That you did," was my response to Tim. I asked Tim "What do you think is going to happen if you keep writing essays like this?" A big smile came across Tim's face and he said "I am going to spend a lot of time in your office."

Fortunately, I knew Tim as a student and I was confident that this was a one-off. What was very pleasing was that the teacher was thoughtful and worried enough to act to ensure that everything was alright and whose ongoing action was to keep an eye on Tim's future work. It did make me wonder what Steven King was like as a student.

- **Drama** – in Drama students can act out what they are feeling and their actions can give us a clue that something is not quite right for them.

The playing of music can give us clues as to how a student is going. Why is it that a student comes into a lesson and wants to play in an angry and loud style which is out of character for them?

- **Physical Education** – why is it that a student is angry or deliberately hurting other students in the lesson?

Case study – a build up of anger resulting in an outburst

A 12-year-old boy who was in his third week at school was in my class for the last lesson of the day. Out of character the student lost control and hit another student during a game of basketball. The student was sat out to calm down. At the end of the lesson I spoke to the student about his behaviour and through my questioning I learnt the following:

The boy was late to school due to his younger brother not getting ready and he was told off by his teacher who did not care that it was not his fault that he was late. As a result of this, he was late to the next class and again told off. In frustration he muttered under his breath which resulted in being asked to return to see the teacher at recess time.

This did not go well and again the boy was late to the next class, which was a test; the test went poorly, further upsetting the student. At lunchtime there was a disagreement between the boy and peers when playing football which led to further teacher intervention. Again, he was late to the next class as a teacher was talking to the boy. Upon arrival into class the boy was told off and not given a chance to explain himself. Finally . . .

the boy arrived into my class, late.

When I sat next to the boy at the end of the lesson to ask about what had happened he burst into tears. "This has been the worst day of my life," were his words. A series of events had triggered the behaviour. I asked the boy if I could speak to his teachers on his behalf to which he agreed. When I explained the scenario to his teachers via email his teachers all spoke to the boy to ensure that he was okay.

I met with the boy in my role as the school counsellor and together we developed strategies to ensure that there would not be a repeat of the behaviour. Unfortunately, we could not control the younger brother and being late was an ongoing battle, However, this was eventually solved by the boy catching a bus to school.

In the busyness of a school day we can react to the behaviour without taking the time to identify the cause. When we know the cause, our reactions can be very different. This was a case where one event after another lead to an angry reaction.

- **Appearance** – a student's appearance can give us clues as to whether we need to enquire about their well-being. For example, a student who always wears a long-sleeved jumper when the temperature is very hot should cause concern for staff. If a student does not get changed to do Physical Education lessons this should lead to some questions being asked, or why is it a student seems to be losing weight? When we notice some irregularities in behaviour we can ask to check that the student is okay.
- **Clothing choices** – why is a student choosing to wear the clothes they do? I will often ask students who continually break the school uniform rules as to why they choose to do so. What is the cause? Is it to seek attention, difficulties at home or something else?

The choice of clothing may be a signal that something is not right.

- **Not wanting to go on school camps/excursions** – this is a time when the reasons why need to be discovered. The fact that a student does not want to go must be explored.

Case study – identifying fears through questioning

A 7-year-old boy did not want to attend a school camp for one night and his mother alerted the teacher to the concerns of the boy. The teacher, through very careful questioning, discovered that the boy was scared that his parents would separate when he was not there. The boy had heard his parents have a fight and his grandparents had recently separated. The boy's reasoning was that because his parents had argued, they would separate and it would be when he was not there.

Some reassurance from his parents made the difference, but this could only happen once the reason as to why the boy did not want to go had been established.

- **Anger** – anger is a very easy identifiable cue for counselling to occur. Anger will be discussed later in the book (see page 83).
- **Meltdowns** – when a student is overwhelmed a meltdown can occur. Again, this is easily identified and counselling is needed to work on prevention strategies.
- **Disruptive behaviour** – a lot of counselling is used as part of a behaviour management programme. The teaching of strategies to control impulses and the disruptive behaviours is done through counselling techniques.
- **Attention seeking** – negative attention is better than no attention; for some students negative behaviour is displayed to get attention. The negative behaviours are a cue that some counselling may be needed to address the causes of the behaviour.
- **Friends** – students can alert teachers to concerns regarding their friends. Through social media or talking, students become concerned about their friends and subsequently report this to teachers.
- **Friendship group change** – students changing friendship groups or being dropped from a friendship group can cause behavioural change in a student. Counselling can be used to assist the student to cope with the changes.
- **Parents** – parents are always a good source of information. Often parents will alert teachers to concerns about their children, which will require some counselling. A challenge for teachers is when parents say "Please don't tell . . . that I have told you this and can you please talk to them about it."

In my day-to-day work as a psychologist I will often ask students why their parents are worried about them or why their parents have brought them in to see me. It is not unusual for students to be brought in to see me without their parents telling them or explaining the reason for the appointment. Depending on the age of the student this can make the counselling process challenging. However, it must be remembered that the parents are caring of their children and want them to be happy. Give me parents who care and who are seeking help for their children any day over parents who can't be bothered to seek help.

Always welcome parents' concerns.

- **Teachers** – teachers are a great source of information and concerns can be shared to establish if a student may need some support.

There are many clues to tell us that a student may need some counselling but only rarely do I recommend that we react instantly with counselling. The only times when I would immediately sit down with a student is when they are crying or angry and that is to diffuse or finish a meltdown, or when there is a concern about self-harming or hurting others. On most occasions I encourage teachers to get background information about the student from as many sources as possible to establish if there is a pattern to the behaviour, or identify the frequency or cause.

Learning about a student

We have now established that a student is showing behaviours that warrant us sitting down and having a discussion/counselling session to check that the student is okay. Before we do this, it is very helpful to get as much background information about the student as possible.

Getting background information allows us to learn about the interests of the student, typical behaviours of the student, friendships, family history and possibly any cause of the behaviour. Background information can be gained through school files and other teachers. A starting point may be to ask fellow teachers if they have noticed any behaviours and to look at keeping some records to establish if there was a pattern to the behaviour.

Case study – understanding and adapting to the needs of a student

A 9-year-old girl was suddenly very tired at school, her work was not being finished and she had been late for the last five days. It was not until parents were contacted that the reason became evident. The family had visitors staying from overseas and the girl had given up her bedroom to the visitors meaning that she was sleeping on the couch. Every night during the visit, extended family were coming over and the girl was not getting to bed until very late. The outcome was a very tired 9-year-old. The solution was that the school let the girl have a nap after lunch whilst the visitors stayed.

A common question asked when getting background information is "Do I ring and ask the parents?" My response to this question is always that it depends on the severity of the behaviour being addressed. If a student is hurting other students, disrupting the learning of others or is at risk of hurting themselves the answer is always yes. However, if the behaviour can be discussed first with the student without involving the parents, then do so. Where possible, parent support and involvement in the counselling process is encouraged but as students reach adolescence this changes as generally adolescents don't want parents to know too much at all. My advice is always keep yourself safe and do what you believe is in the best interests of the student. If in doubt, talk about your concerns with school leadership.

Background information allows us to learn about a student and get information about the possible causes of the behaviours. This information helps in building rapport quickly but also assists in guiding our counselling session.

Helping a student to tell their story

A challenge for anyone working in the counselling field is the ability to be able to get a student to open up and talk about what is happening that is causing a behaviour to occur.

Sometimes this can be quite challenging because if a student does not want to open up and talk there is very little that we can do to help them.

How can we help students to open up and talk?

There are a number of prompts/tools that we can use to help students open up and talk. I have included a number that I like to use in the Appendix at the end of the book. What we must be thoughtful of is what prompts we use when working with older students compared to working with younger students and whether we need to use prompts at all.

For younger students I will often sit on the floor and work together solving a jigsaw puzzle whilst we talk. I will also use a poster which has lot of different faces and I will ask the student to pick the faces which reflect how they are feeling at the present moment. For very young students I will use three faces and then read a list of words, letting the student pick a face that best relates to the word I say. All of these techniques give clues as to what is impacting upon the student. The faces and words are listed in the Appendix.

For older students I will also use the face poster, but in addition I use a set of cards that have a wide range of pictures of people, scenery, weather, events and faces. Students can pick five cards that reflect how they are feeling. Another option is to place pictures on cards on the floor. A student can choose the pictures that reflect how they are feeling. There are many counselling resources online; however, I recommend St Lukes as a good resource for cards and tools. The web address for St Lukes is https://innovativeresources.org/

Depending on my relationship with the student and the willingness of the student to talk I will make a decision as to whether I will use a prompt to get the student talking. One tool I highly recommend using is a whiteboard as I find that when students can write or draw it helps them to open up. Sitting back and looking at items written on a whiteboard allows a person to reflect much easier. The counselling process is also easier as everything that is being discussed is in front of you. At the end of the session a photo can be taken with a phone or tablet to keep as a record. It can also be photographed by the student to remind them of what it is they are trying to achieve.

Here is a photo of a typical whiteboard of a counselling session for a student who had been getting angry and reacting impulsively and hurting others.

Figure 1 shows a whiteboard session for an 8-year-old student who was having difficulty in controlling his anger and responses to anger. A challenge was to help the student to step back from his anger but also not to respond by hitting other students. The student identified some positive behaviours but also behaviours that needed to be worked on. Ideas to help were then discussed and written up to look at. For example, N.P.C. is written on a student's hand and it stands for No Physical Contact. Using a visual cue helps the student to see their behaviours but also to remember what they are working on.

Before working with a student I will very quickly try to get an idea of what is likely to establish rapport quickly, but also what is likely to relax the student so they feel comfortable to open up and talk. For some students, I will not sit down and engage them at the start; rather I will give them a challenge such as completing a puzzle whilst I tidy up or type on the computer. As we are both engaged doing something the conversation can begin. The paper jet challenge is a favourite in my office, as is the playing of the game *Bloons Defence Tower 4* on the computer. As students complete these activities we talk, but also keep a record of their progress. I did have a parent tell me that her child loved coming to visit me to have a chat but also that her son wanted to be the office record holder for the paper jet challenge (he achieved his goal).

The important thing to remember is that we can't always get students to talk; however, through our actions we can show them that we care and that the door is always open should they ever want to come in to have a chat.

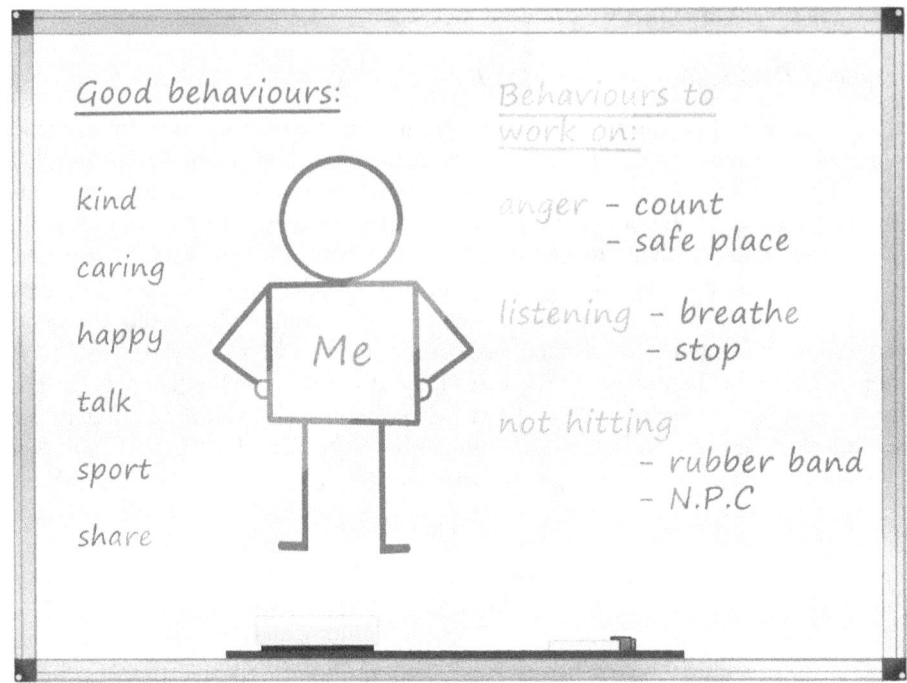

Figure 1 Example of working on a whiteboard

Record-keeping

Whenever we sit and talk to a student in a formal setting it is important that we keep records of the conversation. I would also recommend that if a student tells you something in passing that is relevant to their well-being we should also make a note of it. In today's world technology allows us to do this so quickly. A quick note dictated into a mobile phone or tablet takes no time at all but then allows us to remember what was said.

In regard to record-keeping I see keeping good records as part of 'keeping yourself safe' when counselling. I will keep referring to this throughout the book but I cannot stress enough how we must always keep ourselves safe when counselling. Our notes/records provide us information on what we are working on, what has been said and the dates of our meetings. The worst-case scenario for a teacher is that we are asked to provide evidence in a court of law or alternatively our notes are subpoenaed. Please don't be scared by this but use this information as a reminder of why we need to keep notes and records. It must also be remembered that it is important to know the legal requirements in regard to note-keeping for your workplace and adhere to them. In Australia, for example, notes must be kept until a student is 21 years old.

Just on this, security is also important so notes must be locked away in a safe place or stored on a computer with good security. In a paperless society a well-protected computer system with information backed up to a secured hard drive is what I recommend. Writing notes by hand, scanning them and then storing the file works particularly well as I find students and people in general don't really like the idea of a person typing when they are talking: it seems to depersonalise the whole process. Unless you can touch type, too much time is spent looking down at the screen rather than at the person. Write notes on a piece of paper or whiteboard and then fill in the gaps at the end of the session.

When starting a counselling session, I normally ask the client if it is okay that I make some notes or use a whiteboard. I sit with a clipboard and a piece of paper on my left knee (I am left handed) and write key words in my own special shorthand that I understand. At the end of the session I write up my notes.

Within the Appendix is a sample note keeping sheet that I use to write up my notes.

Before the next session with a student I read my notes and prepare for the review of the plan we had been working on. If using a whiteboard, I will write up a review to look at as a starting point. Having a whiteboard to work on is so very helpful.

Record keeping is a necessary part of counselling from a legal perspective but foremost to help us to be clear about the presenting issues of a student and the processes we are working on to help them.

Maintaining confidentiality

Confidentiality is a big part of counselling but also a challenging one, as often maintaining confidentiality in a school can cause conflict between the counsellor and fellow teaching staff. However, many schools now have systems in place to ensure all the parties in the counselling process are considered (safety) whilst confidentiality is kept.

What is confidentiality?

I try and keep this definition very simple. Confidentiality to me is not sharing another person's personal information with another person. Very simple and it is easy to get bogged down in definitions; however, this gives you the basic idea.

Why is confidentiality important in a counselling relationship?

Confidentiality is important because it forms trust between a counsellor and a student. A student can feel as though they can say anything that is important to them to the counsellor because they know that the counsellor is trying to help them, but also that the counsellor will not be sharing the information with anyone.

Why can maintaining confidentiality in a school be challenging?

Within a school maintaining confidentiality can be a challenge, as teachers, who are caring by nature, often want to know what is happening with a student or why a student wasn't in their class. It can become a bigger challenge when the teacher is the cause of the student's concern.

Case study – conflict in boundaries within a school

A Year 7 student reported to me that a teacher would often call students imbeciles or idiots in jest when a poor answer was given. The teacher, who was a very experienced and popular teacher with the students, would crack jokes, laugh with the students but

(continued)

(continued)

every now and then he would call a student a name in what he would perceive to be fun. However, a student reported to the counsellor that he did not like it.

The counsellor met with the teacher and gently raised the concern. The response from the teacher was "Who was it, who is the student?" The response from the counsellor centred around following confidentiality and the student's name was not disclosed. This infuriated the teacher.

It was reported back to the counsellor that the teacher was then complaining to fellow staff members about the actions of the counsellor in not disclosing the name of the student. Given the teacher was popular with students and colleagues this then made the staff room environment somewhat uncomfortable for the counsellor.

The important point was that the teacher stopped the behaviour. This is a classic scenario where counselling and keeping confidentiality is challenging because the cost in doing so can result in isolation from peers.

Within schools I always encourage counsellors to actively visit staff rooms and to become a part of the school community whilst remembering that professional boundaries must be maintained. Visiting the school staff room also allows easy communication with teachers; on many occasions I would ask teachers how a student was getting on in their class.

When must confidentiality be broken?

Within an educational setting there are many Acts which must be adhered to in regard to child welfare and safety. These Acts must always be followed as that is the law. Professional development also needs to be completed to ensure teachers and school staff fully understand the processes of how to report to authorities when a child's welfare and safety are compromised.

If a student tells you any information where a report needs to be made, confidentiality is immediately broken. This process must be made clear to teachers and school staff. Where the confusion arises is when the student is providing information about themself or another student where a behaviour or action will lead to harm of a person.

As a psychology student I vividly remember learning about confidentiality and in particular a statement that I continually refer to when thinking about confidentiality. The statement is *if you believe a student is going to hurt themself or someone else as a result of their actions you must break confidentiality.*

Case study – breaking confidentiality

On a Friday afternoon after school a student walks into my office to tell me that a student has said that he is going to kill himself on the weekend. Frantically I run around the school looking for the student, without success. Applying the rules of the statement above, I believe that a student is going to hurt themself so I must break all confidentiality. As a result, I need to ring the parents of the student who has expressed suicidal thoughts. As you can imagine this is a very hard phone call to make; however, it needs to be made.

The parents were very shocked but grateful that I phoned and kindly phoned me later in the evening to let me know that everything was okay and it was a throwaway line made by their son in regard to a poor result in a maths test. A hard phone call to make but I always reflect upon the possible scenario where I did not make the phone call and the boy did hurt himself.

As a side point, I always say to counsellors that you must ring and talk rather than email. A phone call can be followed up with an email.

Within a school setting if you are ever unsure or uncomfortable in breaking confidentiality please talk immediately to senior staff, the school counsellor or a person who can help you. The fear many teachers report to me is that they will lose the relationship with a student if they break confidentiality and thus the counselling will end. How can we break confidentiality whilst maintaining the counselling relationship?

Talking to students about confidentiality and how to gain support

I always ask teachers as to why they believe a student is presenting for counselling and in nearly every case the answer is because the student wants help. This thought can be used to guide our thinking on confidentiality. In regard to talking to students about confidentiality I encourage a common-sense approach based on your experiences with a student, background information and the relationship you have with a student.

There is a school of thought that suggests that students need to be informed about confidentiality before any counselling occurs. How do you think this looks? You have asked to meet with a student because you have identified that they have become very withdrawn. The student arrives and sits down in your office. The first words you speak to the student are "If you say anything to me and I think that you are going to hurt yourself or someone else as a result of your actions I must break confidentiality." How do you think a student would feel about this? Not a great way to start a conversation, is my thought.

To me, common sense suggests that you establish rapport with the student and begin the counselling process, remembering full well that it may be necessary to stop the session to talk to the student about confidentiality and the legal requirements that need to be met as a teacher. The age and understanding of a student must also be considered when talking about confidentiality.

What happens to a counselling relationship when confidentiality is broken?

We must remember that the reason a student is talking to us is because we have identified a concern or a student has approached us seeking help. If we have developed a good rapport/relationship with the student it is likely that breaking confidentiality will not harm the counselling relationship. The challenge is to explain the process to the student so they are very clear that our intention is to help them to the best of our ability.

Case study – confidentiality in a counselling relationship

A 13-year-old girl presents very upset, withdrawn and frustrated that she has been embarrassed by a teacher in front of her peers for not doing as well as normal in a test. Upon talking to the girl, it was disclosed that home life was very unstable with her parents fighting on a nightly basis and that her father had indicated an intention to move out. In talking to the girl, it was decided that confidentiality should be broken and that as the school counsellor I would contact all of the girl's teachers to explain what was happening.

Together the girl and I constructed the following email to teachers:

> Dear staff
>
> Emily Smith in your Year 9 class has met with me and indicated that she is having great difficulty at present keeping up with her workload due to some emotionally challenging external factors. I would ask that you modify your expectations of Emily in regard to her class and homework.
>
> If you have any questions regarding Emily please talk to me directly rather than approach Emily in the classroom. I will advise of Emily's progress.

In this scenario I talked through with Emily the benefits of breaking confidentiality and letting her teachers know that she was finding it hard to keep up with her work due to what was happening at home. The staff could then play their part in supporting Emily without knowing the reasons as to what was happening.

It must be never be forgotten that our goal is to help students through the processing of counselling. If the worst-case scenario is that a student no longer wants to work with you due to confidentiality being broken that is okay; most importantly, the process of getting further help to support the student has begun. In my experience, when a good relationship exists the counselling process will not cease due to confidentiality be broken – rather it strengthens because the student understands how you are doing everything possible and necessary to help them.

Keeping yourself safe / discussions with leadership

When working in a counselling role within school it is so important to keep yourself safe. Student confidentiality is paramount but at times it is necessary to talk to the school leadership teams to debrief – especially if a student could cause harm to themselves or another person. Having a regular meeting with a school leadership team member to debrief and discuss any presenting issues allows the opportunity to seek an alternative perspective but also alerts school leaders to any potential challenges that could present.

As a part of keeping yourself safe I also encourage that a network is set up with people from a wide range of schools who work in similar roles, and that you meet on a regular basis. This allows the opportunity for professional development, discussion of cases (without names) and also the development of contacts between schools. This is useful given the large interaction between students attending different schools through social media.

Confidentiality is important; however, keeping yourself safe whilst doing the best you possibly can to help a student is vital.

The setting for counselling

Never underestimate the power of the first impression!

Put yourself in the position of the student walking into a room for counselling. What words come to mind to describe how you are feeling – especially if this is the first time you have gone to seek some help. Words like *scared*, *apprehensive*, *confused* and *nervous* come to mind. So, what can we do to help a student feel at ease?

The first impression is critical and it starts with the greeting and the setting of the room.

When greeting a student always use their name and smile. Welcome them into your room. It is what the student now sees that can make a huge difference in whether they relax or maintain their nervousness. What does a good room look like? What is it that will help a student feel at ease?

I am not an interior designer; far from it. However, I have worked out over time that the following items can make a big difference:

- **Comfortable chairs, beanbags or stools** – somewhere inviting to sit.
- **Soft toys** – I had a teddy bear in my office and 95% of the students who sat down hugged the bear whilst talking.
- **Puzzles** – items for students to play with whilst talking.
- **Posters** – things for students to look at that are of interest and create discussion.
- **Juggling balls** – I had three Simpsons juggling balls and this created a discussion point, but it also allowed me to teach the student to juggle.
- **Old photos** – students like looking at old photos; it also creates a discussion point.
- **Fish** – students will look at the fish and feed them. Any animal is good and I once met a teacher who had a snake – kids loved it.
- **Trophies or certificates of achievement outside of school** – again, it creates a discussion point.

Put yourself in the position of a student. What room do you want to walk into? A room that has some posters, trophies, juggling balls, teddy bears, beanbags, etc., or a room that has a poster describing the harms of smoking, drinking, bullying, etc. with two chairs and a coffee table between them.

I know it is not always possible to have the best environment for counselling but give it some thought as the setting helps to calm the student and reduce their initial apprehensions.

Something to also consider is having a sign on the door alerting people that there is a counselling session in progress and asking them to please knock and wait. It is difficult in today's world in regard to personal safety and the idea of being isolated in a room with a student can be a scary proposition for any teacher, particularly a young male teacher with older female students. Keeping yourself safe is important and I advise teachers to look at the setting of the room. Is there a window so people can see in? Are there blinds, so again people can see in but not see the student? Does the door need to be left open a little bit for personal safety? All of these things must be considered.

My advice to teachers is before sitting down to talk with a student, get as much background information as possible on them. If you know the student and have a sense of safety you may feel comfortable working with the door closed. If you have information regarding serious allegations about other teachers made by a student then I would recommend having a meeting with another teacher present. Your judgement and gut feeling must be trusted. Remember, if at any time you don't feel safe, stop the session.

Figure 2 An example of a welcoming office

Figure 3 A good example of an office that has lots of interesting things in it

Hole in the door

Setting means for communication between students and teachers is important. In today's world an email is an easy way for a student to let a teacher know that they would like to chat. Alternatively, having a small slot in the door for a student to put a note in can also alert a teacher that a student wants to talk. This works well if a counselling session is occurring and a student wants to talk at the same time. A notepad outside and a pencil allows the student to write a quick note, which is then placed through the hole in the door and into a tray attached on the other side. The teacher can then respond to the note at the end of the session. This allows communication whilst not disrupting the session which is in progress.

Access – alleviating students' feelings of embarrassment

When working with adolescents, particularly boys, we need to be aware of students being embarrassed about the idea of having counselling. Unfortunately, there is still a stigma about it and for many teenage boys having counselling is perceived as a sign of weakness. I am pleased to say that this perception is slowly changing but we still have a long way to go.

The *Mission Australia Youth Mental Health Report* conducted in 2016 indicated the female teenagers were more likely than male teenagers to seek support through a school counsellor, whilst males were more likely than females to seek support through an outside community group.

We can help students by doing the following things:

- Having different entry pathways to the counselling area allows students to access the counselling space without being seen by their peers.
- Having counselling sessions before or after school.
- Planning sessions after recess or lunch as this allows students to head straight to the counselling area rather than go to class first.
- Teaching students what to say to their peers if they are asked about where they were or why they went to a meeting with a teacher or school counsellor.

This last point is very important. I encourage the teaching of what I call a "GEL", which stands for a Graceful Exit Line. Some GEL examples might be:

- "Just had to talk to Mr Smith re football training this week."
- "I have to go to a dental appointment so got to leave at the end of recess."
- "I am having a few hassles at home and Mr Smith is helping me with it."

The key point is that we teach students ways to deflect any embarrassment they may feel with their peers about meeting with a teacher or school counsellor.

Body language – set up, greeting and the importance of the initial presentation

As previously pointed out, the initial greeting is of great importance. Students need to feel welcomed, as more often than not they are apprehensive about commencing a counselling relationship. When first meeting a student, the following strategies can be used to help to establish rapport very quickly:

- Smile.
- Use the student's name when greeting them.
- Invite them into the room.
- Have an activity ready to go if needed.
- Draw on knowledge of the student gained from background information to ask initial rapport-building questions.

Case study – making students feel comfortable

When working with younger students I will often talk to parents to find out information relevant to helping the student. Whilst talking to parents, my assistant Tina will sit with students whilst they do a drawing or some colouring in. The finished pictures are stuck to our cupboard for students to see.

At the end of the session the picture is added to the file of the student and on the day of a subsequent appointment the picture the student has done is removed from the file and reattached to the cupboard for the student to see. Little gestures like this makes a student feel welcome and valued.

Making students feel comfortable in counselling is a challenge at times but through a few small actions we can help to reduce the anxiety a student may feel.

Building the counselling relationship

For the majority of students who seek counselling, having a good relationship with the teacher is imperative. For some students the relationship is not as important as the need to have a person to talk to; generally, however, the relationship is of great importance. So how do we build the relationship?

1. Learn about the student

    Before beginning a counselling session, it helps if you can learn as much as possible about the student. This can be done through reading files, asking questions from previous teachers and through asking the student to complete questionnaires. The information gained allows us to ask relationship-building questions about sport, hobbies, music, favourite subjects, etc. It can also allow us as counsellors to share an interest, whether that be in sport or music.

In practice I generally like to talk to parents before meeting with a student so I can get some background information to help me with my rapport-building questions. Some typical rapport-building questions are:

- What school do you go to?
- What house group are you in?
- What are your favourite subjects?
- Are you doing any activities at school?
- Who are your favourite teachers?

2   Be yourself
    Students are good at identifying what my daughters call a "try hard": that is someone who is trying to act cool. It is important to be yourself and use the words and language you would use every day. As teachers, we are not there to be friends with the student, we are there to support and help the student to develop strategies to help themselves. Please don't start using the modern-day terms that students use, but rather show interest and ask what the words mean. Students feel very empowered when they teach us things and this is a good opportunity for them to do so. Be yourself!
3   Acknowledge the student away from counselling
    Students who you are working with appreciate a wave or a nod when you see them but please be discreet. Many students do not want to be embarrassed in front of their peers so please look at the setting, the people around and then consider the possible impact on the student before saying hello. A simple nod of acknowledgement as you walk past in the yard is enough to let the student know you are thinking of them.
    It is also important to remember to keep counselling to the counselling setting. There can be a time for an impromptu counselling session but we must be so aware of time, place and the impact on the student. In the yard at recess time with peers around is not a good time.
4   Follow through
    Students lose respect very quickly when we do not follow through. If we say we are going to do something for a student we must do it. When we follow through, students gain confidence and the counselling relationship builds.
5   Keep in touch
    When the counselling relationship ends it is still important to keep in touch with the student. This can be done by always saying hello to the student or giving a nod at the appropriate time. Students appreciate that you still show interest in them, and as a result of this a student is much more likely to return to seek help should the need arise.

> Word of mouth is very important within the school yard as students talk. If a student has had a good outcome in counselling and a strong counselling relationship has been built students will recommend the teacher to peers as a good person to talk to. A good relationship with students can be gained by going on school camps, attending sport or music performances, acknowledging students' artwork, etc. Students then have a perception that you are approachable and a person who cares about them.

Counselling older and younger students

In many schools we will be asked to work with a wide range of students from various backgrounds and of course who are of different ages. As a result of this we need to be conscious of the differences in approach when working with students of different ages. As well as considering the maturity of the student, some of the key points to remember when working with students of a variety of ages are:

- The language that we use. We must be sure it is appropriate for the student.
- The amount of time taken. More often we will need more time when working with older students.

- The prompts that we use. We must make sure they are appropriate for the age level of the student.
- The seriousness of the issue presenting. As students get older the tendency is for the issues to become more complex; however, we must show the same considerations to students of all ages regardless of the presenting issue.
- The ability to comprehend what is happening but also the strategies we are trying to teach. Younger students will need more time and support when learning new strategies to ensure they know how to apply the strategy.

Case study – working with students of different ages

John, a 16-year-old student who was boarding at a school, had the physique of a fully developed man at the age of 15 and too often he was treated according to how he looked rather than his maturity level. John was often getting into trouble within the boarding house at school for inappropriate behaviours. Upon talking to John, the counsellor realised that although John looked like a fully-grown man, his maturity and behaviours were more like the level of a 12-year-old boy.

The counsellor worked with John to develop a greater understanding of his behaviours and how they were perceived by his peers, but also talked to the staff of the boarding house and school to alert them to John's level of maturity. Looks can be deceiving.

I hope that you now have an understanding of what counselling is and what it is not, how to identify a student that may need support, how to set up the counselling environment, how to build rapport and some ideas about the differences between working with boys and girls. With this knowledge it is time to learn the Solution-Focused Counselling Model.

4 The Solution-Focused Counselling Model

We have now identified that a student is in need of some support, our room is set up, the time has been made and it is now time to talk to a student. The final thing before commencing the session is to have an understanding of a basic Solution-Focused Counselling Model (SFCM) that can be used to guide the session. The model I am going to introduce you to was the first model I ever learnt as a counsellor and I still use it as the base of my sessions 15 years later; the only difference being that I adapt different techniques I have learnt into the model when necessary.

The aim of the SFCM is to provide any counsellor/teacher with a simple process to follow in counselling. The model follows a very simple plan that allows for a student to open up and talk before identifying the changes they would like to see happen. The student is then guided in how to work towards solving the problems that are presenting to them through learning how to brainstorm solutions and then putting the solutions into practice. The encouraging part of the model is that through counselling, we are teaching students how to solve their own problems through a process that can be adapted to suit their individual needs.

> On a side note this is an excellent model to use for self-regulation as well. When I completed my studies, I attended residential schools in Victoria, Australia, meaning I would be away from my wife Katie and children for a week at a time. Within the residential schools we would complete six hours a day of counselling sessions in groups of three with one person being a client, one a counsellor and one an observer. After a week of intensive learning, but also counselling, I would leave feeling very good and with a very clear head.
>
> Upon returning and settling into everyday life the stress would occasionally catch up with me, to which my wife would say "You need to go back to Victoria and work on that model you learnt!" How right she was, as when I would then reflect and work through the model I would eventually solve the stress on my mind.
>
> "Look after the self" is a big mantra of mine and applying the model to our own life stress is a good start.

I am very reticent to use the word *problem* when working with students as I believe that the word has a negative connation to it; this is why the model I recommend is called the Solution-Focused Counselling Model – it has more of a positive note to it.

There is certainly one thing I always say to teachers and that is to always avoid using the P words in counselling. The first P word applies in the opening lines; by that I mean we never open with "What is the problem?". This is because it infers there is a problem when sometimes the student may be wanting to talk through items which are more advice orientated. Please don't open with "What is the problem?". Once a student has told us there is a problem then it is fine to refer to the issue/challenge as a problem because the student has identified it.

Whilst on the topic of P words, the other P word we never use is *promise*. We should never promise anything to a student, particularly when we may not know what the student is going to say. A common thread is a student saying "You have to promise me that you won't tell anyone after I tell you what has happened." Now this is not possible due to confidentiality and duty of care laws that apply. So please, never use *problem* and *promise*.

Here is an outline of the model. I encourage teachers to have the model on their lap when learning how to use it or, alternatively, write the steps down the side of a whiteboard so that information can be written up and recorded when talking to the student.

The aim of the model is to guide students through the process of talking about the concern, identifying the changes they would like to make, creating strategies to make the change happen, learning strategies to facilitate the change and then in how to evaluate the success of the process. It is hoped that by working through the model, a student will learn to become a solution-focused thinker with the skills to solve many of the challenges faced daily by themselves.

Opening lines

Opening lines are the initial words/communication we have with a student. They are greetings but also begin the counselling process. One of the biggest challenges is to make students feel at ease as quickly as possible and how we open our conversation can have a very big impact upon this. Often teachers say to me how they find it hard to get the conversation started. My thought on this is to learn a few opening lines which can be used repetitively.

Here are some possible ways to get the conversation going:

- How are you?
- What has been happening?
- What brings you in to see me?
- How are things going?

If this doesn't get any real response the following can be tried:

- I have noticed that you have been a bit flat lately, is everything okay?
- A teacher noticed that you have not quite been yourself lately, is everything okay?

The use of questionnaires such as the Sentence Completion Test (you can find this in the Appendix) can also be used. Upon arrival the student fills out the questionnaire and then this can lead to talking points. An example might be "I have noticed that you wrote that you are finding school very hard. What is happening at school?"

The most important thing in the opening is to make the student feel relaxed and to give them ways to start the conversation. Once we have the student talking, it then becomes about listening.

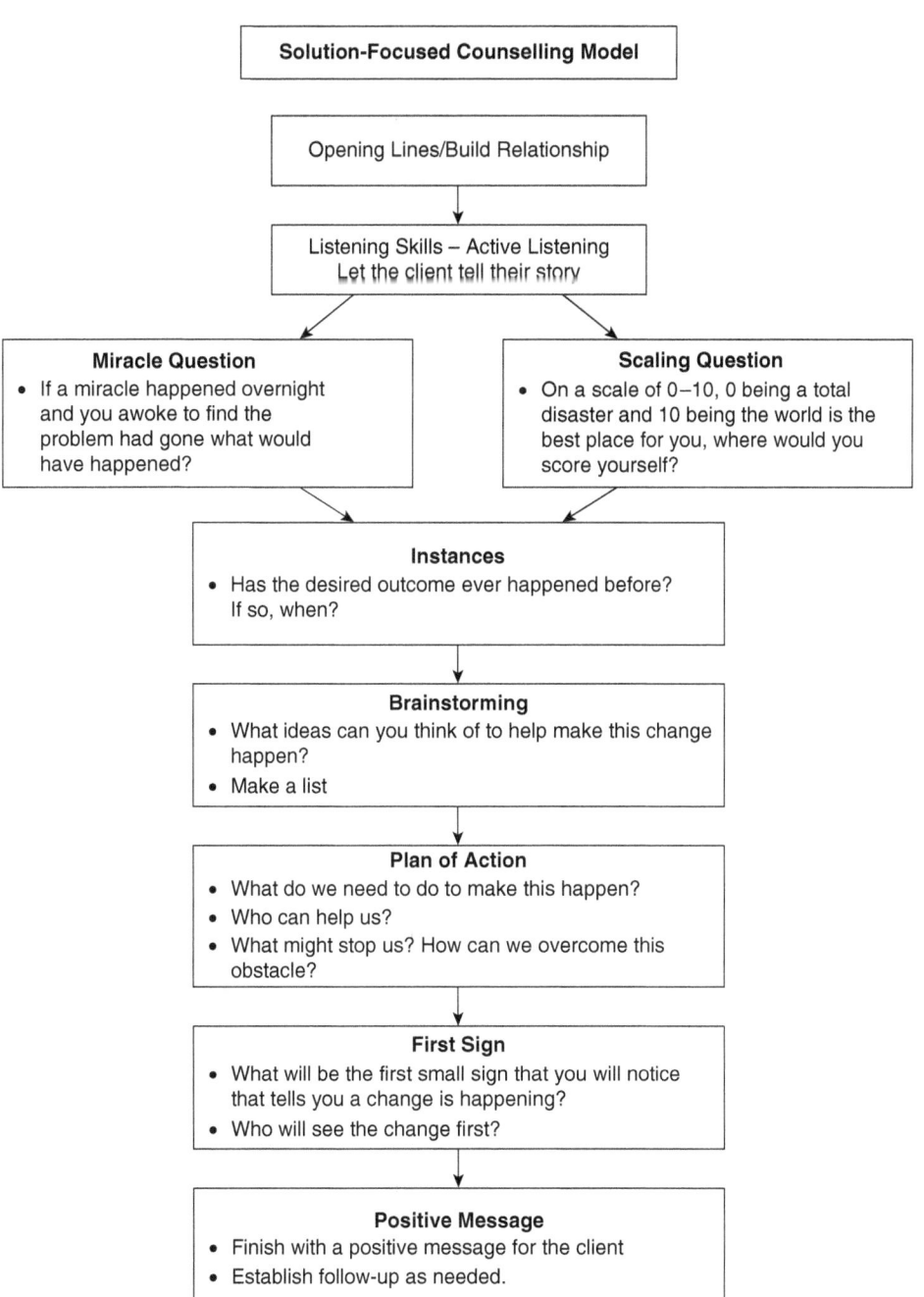

Figure 4 Solution-Focused Counselling Model

Listening – allowing the student to tell their story

It all starts with listening. As I have said, so much of counselling is in the listening. Active listening conveys to the student that we are with them and want to help them. It shows a student that we value them and care.

When listening to students it is our body language, prompting questions and responses that encourage the student to talk more – and remember, silence is a big part of this. The challenge is to find out as much as we can about what has happened, what the student is thinking, how it is impacting upon their behaviour, how long it has been happening for and find out the student's overall level of well-being. This then allows us to determine if a forward referral is needed but also if the student is at risk of self-harm.

Whilst on self-harm it is important to understand that it is okay to ask a student if they have had thoughts about hurting themselves or suicide. It is a hard question, but when necessary it needs to be asked to make sure that a student is safe. Please don't be scared to ask a student if they have had thoughts about hurting themselves; if the answer is yes, this needs to be explored further and confidentiality broken to ensure the student is safe.

When listening we are trying to get as much information from a student as possible.

The following points can be applied when listening:

- **Use lots of verbal prompts** – "yeah", "yes", "um", "okay", etc.
- **Reflecting feelings** – "It sounds to me like you are feeling . . . as a result of . . .." The use of feeling charts/prompts can help students identify feelings.
- **Empathetic understanding** – "It sounds to me like it is a sad situation."
- **Open vs. closed questions** – textbook counselling recommends always using open-ended questions; however, as many teachers would already know when talking to teenage boys, this is not going to work. I always say with teenage boys, one grunt for yes, two for no. I see it as impossible to always ask open-ended questions, so use closed questions but where possible follow up with open-ended questions. An example might be when asking a closed question, it is followed up by "Can you tell me more?" Another idea is to get a student to tell you about how something works or how they achieved something. I also find when working with students who are on the Autism Spectrum that closed questions often work better.
- **Using prompts** – prompts are a very good way to get students talking. Picture cards, puzzles, question sheets, etc. that provide the student with a means to open up and tell us what is happening, how they are feeling.
- **Avoid making judgements or loaded remarks** – when listening it is important not to make loaded remarks or judgements as this will stop the conversation in its tracks. Comments such as "You did what?" are not going to help. We must also not judge a student on their actions or thoughts. The job is to listen and comments such as "That was a dumb thing to do" or "You have got that completely wrong" are not appropriate when listening.
- **Avoid changing the subject** – often counsellors have very good background information and know a lot more than the student realises, but when this is the case it is important to still listen and let the student talk without directing them to what we know. This can come much later and even at follow-up sessions.

- **Avoid speaking too often and for too long** – too often counsellors will talk too much in counselling sessions rather than listen. Be comfortable with silence and work at not talking too much.
- **Clarifying** – during a counselling session there are times when we will lose focus or not really understand what has been said by a student. As a result, it is important that we clarify what has been said. Comments such as "I am not with you on this, can you tell me again?" will allow clarification.
- **Summarising** – at the end of the initial conversation it is good to summarise what has been said. "So, what you're saying is . . ." or "So what has happened is . . . and you are feeling . . . .." are good ways to summarise the conversation before moving on to the problem-solving component.

Again, the use of a whiteboard is very helpful to make notes that can be referred to and used later in the counselling process. This is also the time when I ask the student about taking notes and when I let them know they are happy to read my notes at the end if they would like to.

Identify change

We now have an understanding of what is happening to the student and the impact upon their well-being. The next step is to identify the change a student would like to have occur. This is the beginning of teaching students to think through solutions for themselves rather than have people solve all of their challenges for them.

A point to consider here is that it may be a student has raised a number of points of concern when telling their story. If this is the case, I recommend asking the student which area they would like to address/work on first. This can be done through discussing the scenario that the student believes most needs to be addressed. Having all of the concerns on a whiteboard helps a lot here as the student could score each area out of 10, according to how much of a concern it is to them. This allows the teachers to also get an understanding of the needs of the student.

The next step is to look at the type of questions we ask students that assist them in identifying the change they would like to see happen.

Miracle Question vs. Scaling Question

The focus of the next question is to get the student to tell us what they would like to have happen; this can be done through using a Miracle Question or Scaling Question. Personally, I tend to use Scaling Questions for older students and Miracle Questions for younger students, but they are definitely not exclusive.

Miracle Question

The object of the Miracle Question is to get a student to identify the change that they would like to see happen. A Miracle Question for a younger student would be "If I could wave a magic wand and tomorrow everything was good, what would have changed? What would be different?" For an older student the question would be "If a miracle happened overnight and tomorrow everything was just as you wanted it, what would have happened? What would be different?"

Here are some possible Miracle Questions to ask students.

- If a miracle happened during the night when you were asleep and the next day the problem you had was gone, how will you know the problem has gone?
- What would you be doing differently that you weren't doing before?
- Who else would see this difference?
- If I were to wave a magic wand over your head and say some magic words which caused the problem to go away, how would you know that my magic had worked?
- See yourself in a year from now, what would be different about you as a result of our meeting?
- Who would notice the difference?

The idea is to get the student to identify the changes that they want to have happen.

Case study – helping students to identify changes

A student who was being bullied in the classroom identified that if a miracle occurred overnight the following things would have happened:

- The teacher of her History class would be aware of the behaviour of students and in particular the bullies.
- The bullies would leave her alone.
- She would have more resilience.
- She would have more friends in the class.

From this we were able to identify the items that the student wanted to have changed and then set about working on how we could achieve them.

There will be times when a student might respond with a miracle which is completely unattainable – when this happens we can encourage them to think of other options. For example, if a student has had to move to another school the miracle might be that they would be back at their previous school. This is likely not going to be possible; however, we can then work towards helping the student feel better about being in the new environment and identify the changes that can occur for that to happen.

Scaling Question

Scaling Questions are used to gain an understanding of how much impact the problem is having on a student's well-being. It also allows the counsellor to set a benchmark to track progress, which is also very helpful throughout the counselling process.

A student is asked to rate the problem on a scale from 0–10 with 0 being very challenging and 10 being a little bit challenging. The use of whiteboard certainly helps here as the scales can be written up. After a score is recorded, the student is asked "What would need to happen/change to lift the score up by two points?" The student can then start to identify the changes that would need to occur to help them to improve their situation.

Case study – using scaling to identify change

A student presented as sad as she was feeling left out of a friendship group after not being invited to a party. The girl rated herself as 6/10 on the scale. When asked what would need to change to lift the score to an 8 her answer was "I would get invited to the party." This was explored further and it was decided it was unlikely to happen, so when asked again the girl indicated that she would need some skills to build stronger friendships whilst also looking at who her real friends were.

The girl identified the changes that she would need to make in order to improve the way she was feeling. Scaling works well for older students but it can also be used on younger students provided they understand numbers and the scale is explained well to them. Younger students can have a tendency to rate everything as a 0.

Instances – looking for prior knowledge or experience

Once we have established the changes a student would like to have happen we can then ask the student if they have any skills or ideas that they can use to help make the changes occur. It is possible that a student has thought through some ideas.

Case study – looking for instances

A student has indicated that they are being bullied and have come to the counselling session seeking help. The changes have been identified and the question has been asked as to whether the student has any ideas on what could help with the changes. The student indicated that when he was younger he would imagine that he had a shield around him that would protect him from bullying and this would work.

When asked why this approach could not be used again the student explained that the bullying is much more serious and happening much more often. The student stated that it was like the shield had holes in it.

What was learnt from this was that the student did have some ideas on what could be done to help to prevent the impact of the bullies. Instances allow the counsellor to learn if the student does have any skills already but it also can give an insight into past behaviours.

Brainstorming – create ideas to make change happen

The next step is to brainstorm some ideas that can be put into place to help the student make the necessary changes. Now, this can be very frustrating for the counsellor as generally, through experience, we as counsellors know the best ideas to help make the changes occur; however, this is the time to listen and encourage the student to explore possible solutions. The aim is to teach students to solve their own challenges rather than instantly solve them for them.

The ideas can be funny, not possible and extreme; however, every idea is recorded. Some humour can creep in to the counselling here (I had a student whose idea was that he could call aliens to take the bully away). As counsellors we are encouraging students to think. Once a student has had a good go at making suggestions we can offer one idea and one only. This at least gives the student one realistic idea to work on. If a student does not have any ideas we need to wait and be patient. I have even placed a student on a computer to look up ideas rather than me give them lots of solutions. As I have said, we are trying to create solution-focused thinkers.

Once a student has listed their ideas and we have added one, we can then work through all the ideas and decide what can be worked on.

Case study – brainstorming in counselling

A 13-year-old who is new to the school and finding the transition hard has come to counselling seeking help to develop new friendships. The ideas that were suggested in brainstorming are as follows:

- Don't come to school.
- Move to the school where my friends are.
- Join a sporting team.
- Catch up with my old friends on the weekend.
- Learn how to talk to new people.
- Join a club at school.
- Go to the library at lunchtime.

A counsellor solution was not given as the student had a number of ideas. The ideas chosen to work on were to make sure contact was maintained with old friends, joining a club at school and looking at how to talk to new people.

Plan of Action

The Plan of Action stage is where we teach students the skills they need in order to put their ideas into practice. For the student described in the previous case study this would mean teaching how to meet and greet a new person, what questions to ask and providing information about possible clubs at school. This can take some time and be worked on in counselling sessions, but also given as homework for the student.

A plan of action can also involve the introduction of a number of counselling techniques such as desensitisation, empty chair, mental imagery and positive self-talk which are described in Chapter 5.

Case study – empty chair and positive self-talk

For the student having friendship challenges we could use the empty chair technique as a part of building confidence to talk to a new person. The student would imagine a person is sitting in an empty chair and rehearse the conversation they would have, then put themselves in the position of the person and respond appropriately. A conversation would be rehearsed with the counsellor guiding the student.

Positive self-talk could be used by encouraging the student to reflect upon previous friendships at their old school and then creating a few simple positive phrases to remind themselves of previous success. Some positive statements might be:

- I am a good friend.
- I have made good friendships in the past.
- I have good friends from my previous school.
- I have the skills to talk to people.
- I can play tennis well so I can join the school team.

These statements can be written up or placed onto a mobile phone for a student to see.

The key to the Plan of Action is in the preparation of the student to attempt the ideas that will lead to the desired changes occurring. Sometimes as the counsellor we can assist by talking to teachers to alert them that a student is finding some aspect of school difficult and that they will need some support. In the case above, teachers could help by assisting the student into small group work with like-minded students, or by sitting the student next to other students who may not have made new friends.

First Sign

The idea behind the First Sign is to get the student to picture success and what it looks like. I also like to ask a student "What does success feel like?" – this helps the student to get an idea of success and hopefully this provides more encouragement.

After creating the plan, we ask the student to use some mental imagery to create a picture in their heads and tell us what a successful outcome would look like. An example of this would be to ask a student to close their eyes and create a picture of themselves doing a speech in front of their class. I would ask the student to describe to me the picture they are seeing. Another way of explaining mental imagery is to tell students to imagine watching themselves on television. I would then ask them to tell me what they are seeing.

The following are some First Sign questions:

- What will be the first small sign that you will notice that tells you this change is happening?
- Who will be the first to see that this change is happening?
- When you are talking to some new students, what is the first thing you would have noticed that you did differently and would tell us that you are on track to make your change happen?
- If I were a fly on the wall and I saw you had solved your problem, what would I have heard or seen you doing that would tell me that you were on the right track to starting to resolve what led you to come and see me?

Positive Message

Finally, we finish the session with a Positive Message and I honestly believe that this is the second most important part of the counselling process behind the initial contact. This is the time where we make a student feel positive and wanting to leave the safety of the counselling room to go out and have a go at implementing the changes they want.

A Positive Message might be "I am really pleased that you came in to see me and that you are keen to have a go at making these changes. I can't wait to see you tomorrow so you can tell me how everything went."

The idea is to let the student know that we are really supporting them and want them to succeed. The positive message is usually given after a follow-up appointment has been made.

Follow-up session

The follow-up counselling session is very important as it allows the counsellor a chance to talk to the student and to hear about how the student went in implementing the changes. It is also the time for the counsellor to focus on a success the student had attempting the change. Sometimes even the smallest successes are worth noting.

On one occasion I recall the only success I could find was that the student was willing to come back and continue working with me as the student's attempt had gone quite badly. They had tried to talk to a person on the bus ride home from school with the person asking them quite abruptly to stop talking so they could listen to music. However, we were able to build from this.

An example of some of the questions asked in the follow-up session are:

- How did you go?
- What worked well?
- What didn't go so well?
- What area/skill do you need to work on?
- What can I do to help you more?
- Is there anyone else who could help you?

The idea in the follow-up session is to teach evaluation skills to the student so they can learn to evaluate what they did and how it went, but to also then focus on the next step/stage of achieving the desired solution.

The follow-up session and sessions are about evaluation, learning more and more skills and working towards completing the desired outcome. It may also be the time to commence working on a secondary problem a student was experiencing.

Ending the counselling relationship

A common challenge for many teachers who work in counselling roles is ending the counselling relationship. Not ending the relationship when required can result in the student developing a dependence on the teacher and this is unhealthy for both parties.

As a student learns the skills to solve challenges and they appear to make progress, the length of time between sessions can be extended. At the commencement of counselling I recommend meetings as often as possible (daily) but after approximately four meetings

I suggest that the frequency is reduced, with meetings being had every second day, then weekly and finally monthly before the counselling relationship is stopped.

If a student achieves the desired outcome and appears to be happy with what is happening the relationship can end. A Scaling Question here allows the counsellor to get an indication of progress. A statement such as "It looks to me like you have sorted things out and are now much happier" is a good start, before saying "How about we don't make any further appointments but remember I will be here if you need me?"

Conversely, if a student is not making progress this would be the time to seek external professional help and this would be discussed with the student/parents, depending on the age of the student.

As I have said from the beginning, the idea is to help students to become solution-focused thinkers who have the skills to work through the challenges they face whilst at school, but also then as adults.

Notes on using the Solution-Focused Counselling Model

It does take time to learn to use the Solution-Focused Counselling Model; however, like most skills it takes practice. One of the things I like the most about the model is that when students return for follow-up sessions you do not have to go through the entire model all over again. This is because you already know the story as the student has told you in your initial meeting. In follow-up meetings we can choose the parts of the model that are needed.

Case study – following up in counselling

The student who is having difficulty transitioning into school returns and indicates that they have joined the tennis team and have made a new friend in their home group class. From here the process would be:

1. Ask a Scaling Question to identify any further changes.
2. Brainstorm some more ideas.
3. Create a Plan of Action and practise a new skill.
4. Give a Positive Message.

The beauty of this model is that it allows counselling time to be significantly cut down and for busy teachers this is vital. Sometimes a new issue will be presented and this must be explored; however, more often than not the follow-up sessions can be shorter and more directed to achieving solutions.

Some points on using the model:

- The order does not need to be adhered to as students can jump from place to place. An example of this is when a student tells us something new midway through the brainstorming stage and the new information needs to be listened to and explored.
- Stages of the model can be skipped once we have listened to the student and got the whole story.

- It is okay to have the model on your knee as a part of your note-taking or on a whiteboard when learning how to use it.
- The model is flexible and techniques and questioning styles can be added to it.
- The model is a guide and sometimes it will not be used at all (grief counselling).

The Solution-Focused Counselling Model still forms the basis of my counselling today and it has done so for the last 15 years. It takes time to learn but through practice it provides a very solid foundation for teachers to use when working with students.

Now what I am going to do, is give you some simple techniques that you can put into your counselling when using the model. In turn, this will help your students to learn some techniques that they can apply when trying to make positive changes.

5 Counselling techniques

The following are counselling techniques which I use every day as a part of the Solution-Focused Counselling Model. The choice of technique will depend completely on the challenge presented and more often than not, a number of the techniques are used together.

- **Desensitisation** – this is the process of gradual exposure to a fear. Desensitisation is a very good process when a student is apprehensive about an event or there is a behavioural outcome that is desired but they are fearful of attempting the process to achieve the behaviour. An example of this might be fear of doing exams.
- **Mental imagery** – this helps a student to create a mental image in their head about what success would look like in a situation. Questions such as "Can you describe what success looks like to me?" or "What would I see you doing if I were watching you and you were succeeding?" The idea is to help the student to create a picture of success.
- **Thought blocking** – this is the process where students are taught how to block out negative thoughts that can create doubt. Giving students visual or sensory cues (rubber band on the wrist) can help to remind them to block the negative thought and then replace it with a positive one.
- **Cognitive restructuring** – this is the process of looking at a student's negative thoughts and teaching them how to restructure the negative thought with a positive thought.
- **Empty chair** – this is one of my favourite techniques, which I use regularly. It is when we challenge a student's thinking by asking them to put themselves in the position of another person. Questions such as "Imagine Jed is sitting in the empty chair here, what do you think he would think or say to your statement? Now go and sit in the chair and become Jed and respond."
    The aim is to get the student to see things from another person's perspective.
- **Role modelling** – this is where as a counsellor we role model behaviours. Some skills in drama are very useful here and the teaching is done through active demonstration of the skills.
- **Positive self-talk** – here we are helping students to create positive self-statements that they can use to remind themselves that they have the skills/strategies to cope with a situation. Using a mobile phone to write some positive statements to remind a person of strategies can help students to think positive, wherever they are. Visual cues are also helpful.
- **Can control vs. can't control** – teaching students to not worry about the things they can't control and rather to focus on working on the things they can control.

An example of this is teaching students to understand that they cannot control many things that will happen to them, e.g. what is in an exam, so focus on what can be controlled. We can't control the behaviour or actions of others but we can control our own behaviours and we can learn to do this well.

- **Deal with fact (DWF)** – one of my favourites. DWF is allowing ourselves to deal with things when they have happened rather than worrying about *what could, what might* or *what if*. It is helping students to set up a support network to deal with events when they happen and worry less about the *what if*. Visual cues also help students to remember DWF.
- **Homework challenges** – the setting of homework challenges to be completed away from the counselling setting is also important. Giving students tasks, such as creating positive self-talk cues or doing some cognitive restructuring, is an important part of the counselling process. I often explain to clients that part of my role is to teach them skills/strategies to cope with situations, and when learning any new skills they need to practise. A sporting or learning a musical instrument analogy helps students to understand the need for practice.

There are many techniques, in fact far too many to get bogged down with. My thinking is to learn and master a few techniques – the ones described above are a good starting point. Here are some examples of how I would use some of the techniques.

A student who is scared of failing exams

Desensitisation – have the student spend the amount of time that it would take to do the exam in the exam room doing practice exams. This helps the student learn to feel comfortable in the environment. Student gets a feeling for the noise, smell, layout of the exam room, etc.

Positive self-talk – review previous history of taking exams and create positive statements based on the previous history, but also the preparation completed for the exam.

Empty chair – ask the student what parents, staff, etc. expect from the exam results. Gain clarity around what the expectation is.

Cognitive restructuring – turn the negative thoughts into positive thoughts. For example, "I am worried that I have not studied all of the topics in the exam" into "I am well prepared as I have studied all of the topics my teachers have given me."

Thought blocking – the student learns to block the negative thoughts by having positive reminders, such as a wall planning chart showing the amount of time that has been put into preparation.

Homework – in this case the homework is predominately studying, but it is also helping the student to balance their time and maintain well-being.

DWF – this is teaching the student to not worry about the *what if* or *what might* but reassuring that they will deal with the fact after the event. The focus is on preparing well so we reduce the worry.

> **A 16-year-old who is scared of making friends**
>
> **Role modelling** – demonstrate how to greet a person and the associated body skills. Teach conversational skills.
>
> **Empty chair** – have practice conversations with a person.
>
> **Cognitive restructuring** – restructure the negative thoughts about the self and look at the positive behaviours a person has. I would often ask the question "Why are you a good friend?"
>
> **Mental imagery** – ask the student to create a picture of themselves talking to a person or being a part of a friendship group.
>
> **Desensitisation** – have practice conversations with people such as supermarket or café staff who are very good at making small talk. Then move towards talking briefly to one person in a safe setting. The use of small achievable steps is required.
>
> **Can control vs. can't control** – we can teach a student to understand that we can't control another person's response but we can control how we approach the person and start conversations.
>
> **DWF** – rather than worry about the *what if*, *what might* or *what could*, focus on the dealing with fact after an attempt has been made to start a conversation.
>
> **Homework** – learn about potential friends. What is it they like, what are their interests? Practise conversational skills whenever possible, even with parents or teachers.

For so many of the challenges that occur for students in schools these techniques are used within the problem-solving model. More often than not a combination of techniques is used but this depends on the age of the student and their ability to learn and implement the skills.

One piece of equipment which helps enormously when teaching or using the techniques is a whiteboard as it allows students and the counsellors to write up their thoughts; students who have a mobile device can also take a photo of the ideas to help with the learning process.

Challenges in counselling – parents, schools

Working in the role of a teacher/counsellor within a school does have its challenges. Maintaining confidentiality from other teachers and parents can place the counsellor in a very isolated position.

Many teachers and school counsellors have indicated to me over the years that working in the role as a counsellor or pastoral carer can be isolating from staff. People have disclosed how many colleagues don't see the work they do as relevant and comments are made such as "You sit around all day just talking to students" or "What you do isn't going to make any difference anyway". Some teachers (more the old-school style of teacher) think that the students just need to toughen up and it is this sort of attitude that makes it very hard for counsellors.

My suggestion is to build a good support network within a school but also outside of a school. Attending conferences and meetings for counsellors helps to build support but also allows the sharing of resources. In a school it is good to look for like-minded people who also care about students and understand how counselling helps. I suggest that you must attend school staff social functions, go to the staff room and communicate openly with staff so that staff members can see you as a colleague who has an important role to play in the school community.

Talking to parents

Another challenge for counsellors is talking to parents. Bearing in mind the rules of confidentiality, some parents get very upset to hear that their child has been talking to the school counsellor and not to them.

Case study – working with parents

A school counsellor was cornered and challenged by the parent of a 16-year-old girl who was very angry that the counsellor had not called her to advise that her daughter had been in for a number of counselling sessions. The parent felt that it was her right to know as the parent.

The counsellor had met with the student who had self-referred due to the stress/anxiety her mother was causing in regard to the amount of study the student was doing compared to socialising. The counsellor had asked the student if she would like them to talk to her mother but the student was very much against this. The mother had found out via the mother of a friend of the student receiving counselling.

The first thing the counsellor did was to move the conversation out of the vision of other students and into a quiet private area. The next thing the counsellor did was to listen to the concerns of the mother without responding much, whilst at the same time encouraging the mother to talk. The counsellor used her listening and questioning skills. Through this, the mother quickly calmed and opened up about the challenges she was having with her daughter.

When the mother had finished talking the counsellor politely explained that it was so good that the daughter was talking to her and how her aim was to help her daughter to work her way through the challenges she was facing. Hearing this, the mother was thankful for the care the counsellor was showing and the situation was diffused.

This was a situation where the mother was able to be calmed down and then listened to, but also be reassured that the counsellor was trying to help her daughter. Unfortunately, there are many situations where this is not the case and for some parents, seeing a counsellor is a sign of weakness and should not happen. When this happens the procedures of confidentiality must be followed; if in doubt, a discussion with the school leadership team can occur for guidance in how to proceed.

Working in a caring role, whether that be as a counsellor or pastoral carer in a school, does have its challenges – particularly when dealing with parents and fellow staff. Seeking out and developing a good support network helps to make many of the challenges easier to deal with, but it can take its toll. Caring for yourself is critical and will be discussed later in the book (see page 99).

Building relationships with professional agencies

A big part of counselling in schools is having a good relationship with a number of health professionals near to the location of the school. At the same time, it also helps if the health professionals are prepared to come into the school to share their expertise with staff and also to build relationships with staff members and the school communities.

Case study – building relationships with external supports

A school counsellor advised me that in her role it was not unusual for some of the senior students to come in to seek advice after having been active sexually, or who were thinking about being sexually active for the first time. The counsellor, having worked in the role for a number of years, had built up a wonderful relationship with the doctors at the local clinic and as a result the students were referred immediately to the clinic. Often the counsellor would walk to the clinic with the students and wait to provide support whilst the student talked to the doctor.

Through having a good relationship with the clinic, the counsellor was always able to ring and get emergency appointments should the need arise.

Having a team of professionals such as psychologist, doctors, nurses, counsellors, etc. allows students to be referred knowing that the professional has experience working with students, but also that the professional will work with the school to best support the student. As a part of this I think it is also very good when the professionals seek the advice of schools when working with students; often a parent's perception is very different to a teacher's perception of what is happening in a school.

I often hear from parents and schools that a student's behaviour at school is perfect and it is only at home when things become challenging. Being able to talk to the school and the counsellor helps me to get a balanced picture of what the student is really like. I also encourage schools to invite the professionals in to observe students as it can give a true picture of the behaviour of a student, rather than just what presents in a 30-minute office interview.

Counselling is about building relationships and having a good relationship with external professionals makes a big difference when working with students. Everyone can be on the same page and know what the treatment plan is to best support the student.

6 Counselling for grief

> Grief is like a very bad cut. It hurts a lot at first but slowly heals leaving a scar that lasts forever.
>
> (Anon)

How true this statement is; I will often write this up on a whiteboard when doing grief counselling with students as it can help students to understand the grief process. Students can relate to getting a cut or an initial pain and then the slow healing process. In some cases, a scar remains as a reminder of the injury/cut. A very good counselling analogy.

I believe grief counselling to be the hardest of all the types of counselling because in so many of the grief scenarios there is no solution. Unlike the Solution-Focused Counselling Model previously described, where the objective is to help students work towards a solution, there is often no solution and only time combined with some counselling support is the way forward. So, what is grief for students and what does it look like?

What is grief?

When asked what grief is, the majority of people will respond with the notion that grief is the response of people when someone dies. Whilst this is true, what we need to understand for our school students is that grief is so much more. Grief is a sense of loss and for our students this can be brought about by change.

Case study – a student who is grieving

A 17-year-old boy, Justin, in his final year of school presented for counselling on the recommendation of his mother. His mother indicated that Justin had become quite withdrawn, lost motivation for his school work, lost motivation to play sport but was happy when he was socialising with his friends. Justin was also drinking alcohol with friends on the weekends which was a concern for his mother.

Justin presented as a friendly student who was quite open about talking about how he was feeling. During our initial conversation Justin described the following events that had happened to him in his final year of schooling:

1   Girlfriend ended their relationship when she started university. They had been together for eight months.
2   Justin's grandfather passed away. Justin indicated that he was not overly close to his grandfather as he lived in another state but he did like his grandfather.
3   Justin did not make a representative basketball team for the first time.
4   Justin's school team won their final game against a bitter rival for the first time in 15 years and this had now ended.
5   Justin felt pressured to decide on a career and he was sad that school was finishing for him.

It was hypothesised by Justin's mother that he was depressed and it was true that he was showing a lot of signs and behaviours associated with depression; however, when talking to Justin and discussing depression he was very certain that he was not depressed. It was when I suggested that it was grief Justin was experiencing and explained what grief is and how it impacts upon people, Justin immediately identified with how he was feeling.

When explaining what grief was to Justin he could identify with all of the losses he had recently experienced but also the loss that was ahead of him in finishing school. Understanding why he was feeling as he was certainly helped Justin and it was then that we started to work through some processes to help him move forward.

Causes of grief

I often ask teachers to list all of the possible causes of grief that they can think of that can impact upon students. Here are some of the ideas:

- Death.
- Loss of friendship.
- Finishing school.
- Failing exams or tests.
- Having difficulty in learning.
- Not meeting parent expectations.
- Losing at sport.
- Not making the desired team.
- Not being selected for a position.
- Moving schools.
- Finishing the year and moving into a new class.
- Injury.
- Illness.
- Parents separating.
- Parents losing employment.
- Parent gaining employment – not home as much.
- Classmate being terminally ill.
- Father's or Mother's Day.

There are many causes of grief for students and as teachers we need to be aware of triggers and events. We can reflect back on the signs and symptoms that present from students to alert us that a student may need some counselling. We can also be aware of significant days, such as an anniversary of an event, Father's or Mother's Day, Grandparents' Day, etc. as triggers for students. When we know a day is approaching that will impact upon a student we can try to prepare as best we can to support the student. Some pre-event counselling can make a large amount of difference.

How people grieve

Before working with people who are grieving, I think it is good to know a little about how people typically grieve so we can then adapt our approach to best meet the needs of the person. Not everyone grieves in the same way and people will always have their own coping mechanisms; however, in my discussions with teachers there are generally some behaviours that are common.

Some of the behaviours that I have seen from adults are:

- Will cry a lot.
- Like to talk.
- Put other people's needs first, neglecting their own.
- Cook and clean.
- Develop obsessive behaviours.
- Eat comfort food.
- Retreat to places of solitude – shed.
- Drink to suppress feelings.
- Go straight back into routine life.
- Demonstrate destructive behaviours.
- Withdraw from friendship groups.
- Dismiss their own feelings.

Teenagers:

- Question their own existence.
- Seek comfort from friends.
- Make changes to their own lives – goals.
- Set about on a cause.
- Use social media to express feelings.
- Withdraw from family and seek comfort from friends.
- Stop completing school work.
- Find it hard to find meaning in tasks such as school work.
- Anger.

Children:

- Show regressive behaviours such as wetting the bed, becoming clingy and crying a lot.
- Fear of being alone or of parents dying.
- Fear of doctors, hospitals.

- Questions.
- Anger.
- Lack of organisation; seem to be lost at times.

Case study – children and grief

A 5-year-old boy was very upset that his grandfather had recently died. The boy's grandfather spent a number of weeks in hospital before dying. What confused the boy was that he had been repeatedly told that you go the doctor and to the hospital when you are sick and then you get better; however, in this case, the boy's grandfather did not get better. The end result was the boy refused to go to the doctor, questioning "Why did the doctor not make Grandpa better?"

In this case I worked with the parents of the boy first, teaching them the language to use and how to talk to their son about going to the doctor and why it was important to go when you are sick. We also worked through how to explain to the boy about Grandpa and what had happened to him.

Doing this certainly helped but as with all people when grieving, it took a little bit of time before the boy was comfortable to go to the doctor.

Knowing how people grieve allows us to adapt our approach and this is important within a school setting. Understanding our students allows us to prepare ourselves so we can provide the best support.

Working with people who are grieving

Working with adults

When working with adults within a school community there some things that we can do that help.

1. Make sure you are clear about time frames as it is possible to be caught out with a person who is talking a lot. Always be upfront about when you need to go to a class or leave the session.
2. Focus on the students. As a school the students are the major concern. If it is felt that a parent is not coping then we must work towards supporting the parent so the child is safe.
3. Help the adult to establish and contact their own external support network. A list of external professionals is very useful here.
4. Reassure the adult that you are happy to communicate with them; however, the students are your priority.
5. Advise fellow staff members who can talk to the adults if required about supporting their children.

We must remember that our primary role is to support our students and whilst we can talk to adults/parents, it is the students who come first.

Working with teenagers

Working with grieving teenagers can be challenging as traditionally boys and girls grieve and express their feelings in very different ways. Some ideas that help are listed here.

1. Support the students who need it the most. This seems quite harsh; however, often teenagers will feel the need to support their friend who is grieving, which is great, but in the counselling setting it is better to have the person alone. I will say that in the first session I will always have the friends with the person but at the start of further sessions I always spend a few minutes with the friends in the room but then politely ask them to leave. This allows more specific counselling to occur. Always ask if this is okay first though.
2. Alert teachers that a student is grieving so work expectations can be altered. This can remove a lot of stress from students.
3. Ask the student lots of questions to get them to open up. Questions such as:
   - What is it you will miss the most?
   - What is the one thing that will always make you smile when remembering?
   - What was the funniest experience you had?
   - What was the worst habit?
   - How long had you been friends?
   - What was the person's favourite movie/song?

   Using closed questions and a whiteboard to write up responses allows a student to reflect.
4. Be happy with silence. Just being there helps.
5. Work with the student to develop a way of remembering. This could be done through music, art, planting a tree or placing a plaque somewhere in the school.
6. Ask a student if there are any ways that we can help? Often it is the little things that a student needs help with such as letting a teacher know that they won't be attending a class or missing a practice.
7. Re-establish routines for the student for attending school, practices, etc. Helping the teenager get back into routines allows them to slowly move forward and get on with their own life.
8. Monitor well-being and be aware of any significant date that may impact upon a student so it can be prepared for.
9. Make sure the student knows that you are there to help and support in any way you can.

Case study – helping teenagers in grief

A school community was grieving over the loss of a 17-year-old student who died in a car accident. To remember the student the year group created a list of all of the student's favourite songs and created a playlist which was then distributed to the year group.

Case study – social media and grief

Teenagers can often need guidance when grieving. Recently I worked with a number of students who had needed to make a decision on how they were going to use the money they had raised through fundraising at school through the year.

Three months before the meeting, Phillip Hughes, a well-known Australian cricketer, was tragically injured and then died whilst playing the game. Through social media many Australian people showed their grief. The students in the group had decided that the money raised was going to go to a charity created to remember Phillip Hughes.

I asked the group "How many of you had ever met or knew Phillip Hughes?". The answer was none. I then asked the group "How many of you know someone that was impacted by the bushfire that devastated the local community very close to the school?" (the school had its campsite destroyed and many homes were lost). Eight out of the ten students put their hands up. I did not need to say any more and the money went towards supporting the families within the community.

It was not wrong of the students to support the Phillip Hughes charity; however, the students needed to think carefully and be guided on what was close to them rather than what was popular on social media at the time.

When working with teenagers I have found it is good to talk in a group to start with but then to work with individuals. Working in a group allows teenagers to support each other but it is the 1:1 sessions where students will feel happier to be more open about how they are feeling and coping. In a group some students will be reluctant to speak up, thus the 1:1 sessions allow a freedom to do so.

Working with children

When working with younger children resources and books can be very helpful, as are drawing material and even puppets. The first thing I recommend is to gain an understanding of the impact the grief is having on a younger student so the counselling can be adapted to best support. Discussions with parents can help here.

The process for working with children is similar to that of working with teenagers; however, the language used needs to be adapted to suit the level of the child. This is where drawing or working with puppets can help. The aim is to get the child to talk about how they are feeling. Some things we can do to support children are:

1. Let them know it is okay to cry and feel sad.
2. Talk about feelings and the different feelings we have.
3. Provide resources so a child can express their feelings – could be a punching bag to get anger out.
4. Work with parents/family to support.

5   Use books to provide information.
6   Establish school routines.
7   Monitor well-being at school.

Whenever we are talking to adults, teenagers or children the most important thing we can do is listen and be there. Grief counselling takes a lot of time and patience and we need to be ready for tears but also repetition. Sometimes just sitting in silence is all we need as the fact that the person knows you care by being there is enough.

The use of clichés

The use of clichés can be very damaging as it can give a student a message that we are not really listening to them, but rather just trying to make them feel better about what has happened. I cannot stress enough that we must not use clichés when working with or talking to students. Here are some things that should never be said to a grieving person:

- "I know how you feel."
- "You can always get a new cat or dog."
- "There are plenty more fish in the sea."
- "I didn't like her anyway."
- "There is always a good side to things."
- "Be strong."
- "Don't cry."
- "You will get over it soon."
- "Everything will work out in the end."
- "You now need to step up and be more responsible."
- "They had a good innings."
- "At least they are not in pain any more."

I am sure there are many more clichés and sayings I have neglected, but the point is that we should not use them; it can do so much more harm than good. Grief counselling is very much about listening and not speaking.

Using a visual model to explain grief feelings

When working with people who are grieving I will often use a model that I draw, which I find helps people to understand why they are feeling the way they are. The model is shown in Figure 5.

Model for grief counselling

The stages explained

When talking to people I will draw this model (Figure 5) and then explain each of the stages. I have found that having a visual allows people to understand why they are feeling as they are. I will use the example of a 16-year-old student, Sam, who has just broken up with his girlfriend after being together for 12 months.

Counselling for grief 59

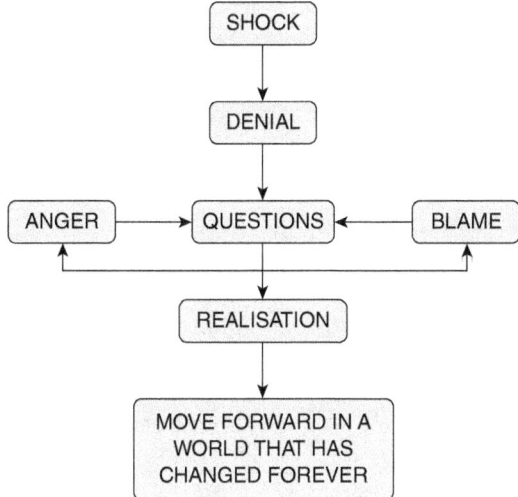

Figure 5 Model for grief counselling

I introduce the model by saying to the student that I am going to draw a model that I think will help him to understand how he is feeling at the moment. With this I write the word *shock*.

SHOCK

Stage 1 is shock; I typically explain that shock is the initial feeling you get when you have just found out the news or learnt what is happening. I ask the following types of questions:

- Where were you when you found out?
- How did you find out?
- Who told you the news?
- What do you remember happening around you?

I will often use the following example.

> I remember working with a student who said that they were watching television and one of their favourite shows when a text came through with some news about a friend who was involved in a car accident. The student explained that they just sat staring at the screen but not watching, not taking anything in that was happening around them.

I then ask the student if they had any feelings like this. Sam replied yes and that his ex-girlfriend asked to meet him for a coffee on a Sunday morning, which was not unusual, where she then broke up with him. Sam explained that after the girl left, he just sat; for how long he did not know. After a period of time Sam went home and cried.

When shock occurs people often explain losing a sense of time, a noise or where they are. It was once described to me as like being in a tunnel with no noise but without an awareness of what was going on around you.

Students understand and relate to these feelings. The level of feelings varies depending on the shock. The next stage is denial.

DENIAL

Denial is a stage where a person shows great difficulty in understanding that a change has occurred. It can take many shapes and forms. Denial is when you have recovered from the initial shock but then expect everything to be the same. Denial is explained through this example. For Sam this was the thought that everything would be okay. His girlfriend would text him later on and they would get back together. Sam was thinking that she was just upset/stressed about school and life but everything would be fine.

An example I use is one of an 80-year-old lady who had been married for 60 years whose husband had recently passed away. Every night for six months the lady set the table for two people and cooked two meals, just as she had been doing for the last 25 years with her husband.

For Sam it was thinking that everything would be okay, the relationship was not over and they would sort things out with the relationship continuing.

ANGER, BLAME AND QUESTIONS

Anger, blame and questions is a stage that students relate to very well. To explain this, I will say it's when you move into a stage where you have a million questions in your head and your thoughts move between being angry and blaming. I will ask "What are some of the questions you have?" "What has made you angry about what has happened?" "Who is to blame for what has happened?"

Sam gave the following responses to the question area:

- Why did we break up?
- Why didn't I see it coming?
- Why didn't I know she was unhappy?
- Is there another guy?
- What did I do?
- Will I ever get another girlfriend who is as good?
- What is it about me?

As you can imagine there are so many questions that Sam had.

When asked what made him angry Sam responded with:

- Not seeing this coming.
- Being too busy with study and sport.
- Not spending enough time with his girlfriend.
- His friends giving him a hard time about his girlfriend.
- The response from his friends after the break up.
- His parents not supporting his relationship.
- The girlfriend's friend.
- School demands.

Finally, Sam was asked who does he blame?

- Himself.
- His girlfriend.
- His friends.
- Her friends.
- Parents.

Through this, Sam was asked lots and lots of questions so he could open up and talk about his feelings and thoughts. Part of this process was getting information from Sam that could be used when helping him to develop new skills to allow him to move forward.

When working on the anger, blame and question stage I also ask students to describe some of the behaviours that they have noticed happening to them. I lead in with the questions "How have you been sleeping?" "Do you find you lay awake at night with a million thoughts going around and around in your head?". Students identify well to this as this is generally what happens. I then ask if they have noticed any other changes. Some typical responses are:

- Crying a lot.
- Not sleeping well or sleeping a lot.
- Moody.
- Get upset over little things.
- Find it hard to concentrate.
- Withdrawal from friendship groups.
- Cease attending social arrangements.
- Not exercising.
- Comfort eating or not eating.
- Lack of motivation to do anything.

As this list is written up on the board I will then ask the student this question: "Do these signs/behaviours present to you as symptoms of a condition that you may have heard of?" The answer is of course yes, with the condition being depression. It is then reinforced to the student that they are not depressed – rather they are grieving but that if we do not work towards helping them through the grief processes, depression can develop. In regard to time frames on this everyone is different; however, I suggest that after six to nine months I would like to see some improvement from the grief.

It is the anger, blame and question stage where I work towards helping the student to understand that it is normal to have feelings of anger and blame whilst having a lot of questions, and as a result they will experience many of the behaviours we have listed. The challenge now is to work towards moving forward.

REALISATION

The realisation stage is often a short stage; it is when the person realises the change is real or final. For Sam this was learning about when he came to the conclusion that the relationship was over. This does not change the anger, blame and questions, or the feelings, but it does help in the next stage which is the moving forward stage.

With Sam, I asked "When did you realise that the relationship was finished and you weren't going to get back together?" Sam explained that after two weeks of no phone contact or social media contact that it was over. Although being a little hopeful, Sam had decided that it was more than likely over and he needed to move forward.

MOVE FORWARD IN A WORLD THAT HAS CHANGED FOREVER

When explaining this stage, I will use the following explanation. I will tell a student that the next step is to move on in a world that has changed forever; that is, their environment has changed forever. You will always have the memories and we can't make these go away but what we can do is to start getting back into routines and begin to move forward.

I will sometimes use the analogy of moving from Windows 9 to the new Windows 10 program. As I say, the software is still there and you know how to use it but there are some new features that you have to get used to using. Some will be good but others difficult to get your head around. I say to students that we are rebooting them into a new version.

To help students move forward I encourage the following things to begin happening as soon as possible and during follow-up visits I monitor what a student has been doing in each of these areas:

1. Exercise.
2. Spending time with positive people. As I say, there are many people who are like dementors (from *Harry Potter*) who just suck the goodness out of you. It is a time to seek out the people who make you laugh and who you have fun with. Students need to be proactive in this stage but having good friends who are aware of the situation also helps.
3. Re-establishing routines. This is going to bed on time, getting up on time, going to school, playing sport, etc.
4. Positive thinking. Helping the student to find positives within themselves and in their day-to-day activities helps.

DEALING WITH THE DREADED BOUNCE BACK

A bounce back happens when you are starting to move forward and all of a sudden you are hit by a memory or see a reminder of what has happened. I illustrate this by drawing an arrow from the moving forward stage back to the anger, blame and question stage. Students understand this and what we can do is teach strategies to help cope with a bounce back. Teaching a student to use graceful exit lines certainly helps.

Bounce backs can be caused by hearing a song, eating a meal at a café, a smell, a movie or television programme, etc. We can make a student aware so they can be somewhat prepared. For Sam a bounce back was inevitable with school formals, friendship group birthday parties and living not far from his ex-girlfriend. Sam was helped by understanding what a bounce back was, but also how he could deal with it. We also worked on how to cope at some of the functions that were ahead for Sam.

When explaining the bounce back I will often tell students how after each bounce back we recover a little faster each time. As I do this, I use the model to show we move through the stages faster each time but we never forget as the memories are etched into our brains. What does happen is the bounce back does not impact upon us as greatly as it did the first time we had one.

When working with the grief model there is still a large element of teaching and helping a student to develop new skills. Like the Solution-Focused Counselling Model, the teaching of skills is a role where as a counsellor we can make a big difference.

When finishing working on the model I will ask a student to take a photo on their phone or write it out on a piece of paper for them to keep. I will encourage the student to look at the model as a reminder that they are grieving and it does take time to heal. It can also help to reassure a student that the feelings they are experiencing are normal; many students have said to me that they think something is really wrong with them when it is actually the strong feelings of grief.

Preparing for grief within a school

It can occur that students within a school will have time to prepare for an event that will cause a grief response. The obvious one is when students leave a school, but there can be occasions such as preparing for a death within a school community where students will require support.

Case study – preparing for grief

A 14-year-old girl, Monica, had a terminal illness and as a result had missed a significant amount of school but was in the process of preparing to return knowing that this was likely to be the last time that she attended school. Through talking to students from within the year group it was discovered that many students were scared not only about what was ahead for Monica but also how to treat Monica and what they should say to Monica.

Upon learning this information, the counsellor organised a meeting with Monica's parents and Monica. From the meeting is was determined that Monica and her family wanted Monica to be treated the same as any other student. It was requested that Monica's peers treat her as they had prior to Monica beginning treatment and it was perfectly okay to ask Monica about her illness and treatment.

With this information the school counsellor sat down with the class and talked about Monica's situation. Monica's closer friends were then asked to come to a meeting with the counsellor where questions were answered from the students but also strategies were taught in how to best support Monica and how to treat her normally. This involved inclusive behaviours whilst also understanding that more often than not Monica may say no to invitations, but the invitations should not cease.

The friends were also involved in preparing items that Monica could take with her as a sign of their friendships. It was also decided that the group would talk to Monica with the counsellor if needed and that in time a decision would be made on how a memorial for Monica could be created within the school.

From this example we can see how many emotions grief creates for students. In Monica's case, the students were scared that they would do or say something to upset Monica and without intervention it may have been that Monica had the perception that no one cared, when this was very far from the case. Preparing students for grief through communicating and teaching strategies does not stop grief from occurring; however, it does help a little.

Finally, with grief counselling an important skill is not being scared to ask for help. It is not unusual for a number of students from a school to be grieving all at once, and when this happens it is good to have some assistance available. This is where having a network of support becomes vital and knowing who can be contacted to visit your school to provide counselling services is imperative. Use your counselling network when needed!

Summary of grief counselling

As quoted at the start of the chapter, *Grief is like a very bad cut, it hurts a lot at first but slowly heals leaving a scar that lasts forever*. As a result of this, grief counselling requires a lot of patience and time with the focus being on listening.

7 Counselling to develop friendships

I didn't realise the extent of how important friendships were to parents until I had my first round of parent interviews as a Year 5 teacher. At the school where I was working Year 5 was an intake year for students, thus there were a number of new students to the school. There were 24 boys in my class and the first questions asked to me by 23 of the boys' parents was about friendships. The other parent asked firstly about Maths scores but then friendships. Most classes have one set of these parents!

When counselling students for friendships I generally start with "What are the qualities of a good friend?". I will then ask a student "How do you demonstrate these qualities?". This is very much like the fly-on-the-wall question – "If I were a fly on the wall watching you be a good friend, what would I see?" I would hope the student would respond with some of the following:

- Listening.
- Not interrupting.
- Being there.
- Sharing.
- Inviting into events/group.
- Not saying negative things.
- Being aware when others are sad.
- Letting a person choose.

I am sure there are many more but once I have established a list from a student I would ask them to rate their skills out of 10 in each area (scaling) and then we would look at how we can improve the skill level in each of the areas. This would then be put into practice.

Another method I have used for older students is the bullseye.

The idea behind the bullseye is for students to identify who their very close friends, close friends and friends are, and then do a quick evaluation of each person within the levels. We establish what qualities are displayed by friends at each level.

As a counsellor I would ask questions such as:

- Why are they a very close friend?
- How do you know the friends in the outer circle?
- What friends could change level?
- What are their good friendship qualities?
- Do they have any negative friendship qualities?
- How much time do you spend with them?
- What is their influence on the friendship group?

66 *Counselling to develop friendships*

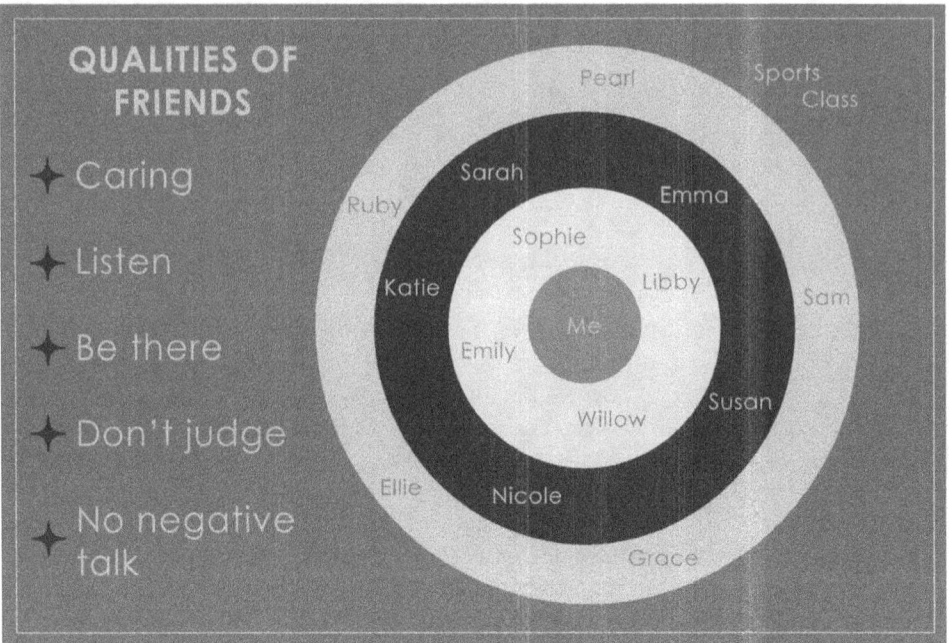

Figure 6 The friendship circle

The idea is to learn about each person at each level and from there we can establish who are positive friends, but also the friendships that we need to develop against the friendships that we should put less effort into. Once this is established, we then work with the student to learn the skills to develop friendships whilst also distancing themselves from some of the other friends.

The idea behind the bullseye is helping students to learn to move friends from level to level. We help students move some friends from *friend* to *close friend* or *very close friend*.

Case study – counselling for friendships

Ellie, an 11-year-old girl who is new to a school, is torn as the initial friends she has made at school upon arrival are quite different to her in their interests. The two friends like Music, Art and Drama whilst the girl loves sport and prefers to be running around playing at recess and lunchtime rather than sitting and talking. Ellie is very aware of her friendships and how kind the two girls have been to her, but she has developed new friends through playing sport at school.

Doing a bullseye, Ellie identified her two friends as close friends but also a number of friends who could easily become very close friends. Ellie resolved to keep her two friends as close friends, but to work towards spending some more time with outer level friends to make them close friends. Ellie, however, was worried about the impact this would have on the current two friends.

The counselling was in helping Ellie work out how she could divide her friendship time. Ellie resolved to spend class time sitting with her two friends but to play with potential new close friends at recess and lunchtime. Ellie would also look at catching up with old and new friends on the weekends.

When counselling for friendship I concentrate hard on ensuring that the student has the skills necessary to build a friendship. Basic body language, listening, sharing, etc. are all important skills that often need to be taught. One of the most common themes I adopt, particularly for adolescents, is **"Don't ever say anything negative about anyone."**

As my mother reiterated to me and my siblings over and over again, "You can think it but you must not say it." Too often students will say something to their peers which comes back to haunt them, whether that be through social media, in a classroom or in the yard. Friendship groups change quickly in schools so it is important that we teach students not to say negative things about anyone at any time. If necessary we work with students to be a good friend and move friendship groups as required.

Case study – teaching staff supporting counsellors

A parent approached a school counsellor worried about her 14-year-old son, Daniel, who had recently shifted his friendship group and moved into a group that was involved in some risk-taking behaviours. This was a difficult scenario for the school counsellor as the behaviours involved were external to the school; however, it was discovered by the school counsellor that the boy's attitude to school, his work and teachers had changed. The challenge for the school counsellor was "How do I address this with the student?"

Rather than approach the boy directly, the counsellor learnt that Daniel enjoyed sport but also the subject of Tech. More importantly the counsellor knew that the Tech teacher was a very good counsellor/mentor for students and as a result of this a discussion was made between the counsellor and Tech teacher about how best to help Daniel. When the moment presented, the Tech teacher took Daniel aside and had a quick conversation with him about his school work and how he was going in general. Daniel admitted that he was struggling and through careful dialogue the Tech teacher suggested that Daniel talk to the school counsellor. The time was made for after school so Daniel's peers would not see him going into the school counsellor's office.

Once talking, Daniel indicated that he felt trapped within the friendship group, restricted by his parent's lack of trust/freedom, was finding school hard and that he had no idea what to do. Daniel admitted that many of his behaviours were out of frustration. Knowing this, the counsellor then began to work with Daniel to address each of the issues. Within the friendship area, Daniel was immediately taught how to use Graceful Exit Lines (GEL) so he did not have to join in any risk-taking behaviours. A bullseye analysis was also done and Daniel was helped to identify some positive friends, but also how to develop some new friendships. A big part of making this change was shifting away from social media.

Within counselling for friendships, I always talk to students about the impact of social media and the information that they present and how that information is perceived by others. Is the information placed purely to seek attention, for humour, to hurt another person? I think we all have friends who post on social media and our immediate reaction is "Why?" or "What on earth are you thinking?" Many of our students need guidance in using social media but also on the impact sharing information can have on friendships.

When building new friendships, I recommend to students that they stay away from social media and work face-to-face. We can teach good social skills which will serve students well for the long-term. As an alternative or addition to counselling at school, students can be referred onto social skills programmes. Having knowledge of agencies or professionals who provide social skills counselling can assist students outside of the school setting to develop skills to make friends.

Counselling for friendships can also be difficult due to the ability of the student to make connections with their peers. For students who have Autism Spectrum Disorder (ASD) this is exceptionally difficult. When counselling an ASD student we must be very clear on the language we use, ensure the student understands what we are trying to teach and we can use a variety of teaching methods. Watching videos, role modelling, scenario training and drama are very helpful when working with an ASD student. At the same time, I also find that humour goes a long way in the counselling relationship.

Whilst on ASD I am a big advocate for social skills groups but also safe places for our ASD students to go to at recess and lunchtimes, where they can meet students who have similar interests. Sharing an interest can be the start of a friendship. Another point is that for ASD students we must look beyond the age of the student – rather we need to look at the interests shared in common. For more information on working with students with ASD I would recommend the following websites:

- Autism Australia – www.autismspectrum.org.au
- Autism Society – www.autism-society.org

Counselling for friendships can be frustrating but also very rewarding. The focus needs to be on helping students to understand what a good friend is and the behaviours associated with being a good friend. Students can then be taught how to demonstrate those behaviours.

8 Counselling for career guidance

The role of teachers within a school is often varied and one of the variations that can occur is being asked to complete some career counselling for students. On many occasions this request is a part of a counselling process; however, in some school settings it is the responsibility of a teacher to provide career counselling for students.

Why is good career counselling necessary? Consider the following case study – unfortunately this is a scenario which I am working with far too frequently in practice.

Case study – career counselling

Jasmine, a 20-year-old, presents as a client having finished her schooling three years ago. During our interview Jasmine reveals that she had finished school and then moved onto university studies; however, she had failed her first three years at university. Through questioning, Jasmine provided the following information to me:

- Jasmine had always struggled with learning at school and she had received learning support throughout her education.
- Jasmine completed subjects in her final year of school that had school-based assessments and no exams.
- Jasmine choose subjects that she felt were easy.
- Jasmine had a tutor who helped her to complete all of her assignment work.
- Jasmine had no idea what she wanted to do when she finished her schooling.

As Jasmine was somewhat unsure of what she wanted to do upon leaving school she was advised by her school counsellor to pick any course that she was interested in, with the mantra being "You can do whatever you want in the world."

Jasmine achieved a good university entrance score and as a result of this she chose to complete studies in Business. This was due to her father owning a real estate franchise and Jasmine thinking it would be good to work in the area after watching what her father did.

Unfortunately for Jasmine, the university course in Business required that students complete Statistics and Accounting in the first year. With no background in the subjects and a dislike of Maths, Jasmine failed both subjects. The same occurred the following year.

(continued)

(continued)

Deciding that Business was no longer a good option, Jasmine decided to study teaching as she liked working with children. Again, Jasmine had to write essays and complete exams which she was not good at and again she failed all of her subjects. The result of all of this was that Jasmine was feeling very worthless and very uncertain about her future.

The first thing that was done to help Jasmine was to identify what her overall level of ability was. As a psychologist I have the testing available to do this. Within a school this is done by looking at past grades, standardised testing results and having discussions with teachers. The next step was to complete a career profile, which indicated Jasmine's interest areas. There are many free online programmes that provide reliable information to students about career interests. From here it was a matter of matching Jasmine's abilities to her areas of interest.

So, what do we learn from Jasmine when doing career counselling?

1. Be realistic – do not recommend subjects or courses for students if you believe they will fail. Do not set students up to fail.
2. Help students choose subjects of interest for their final years of schooling that are relevant to their areas of interest.
3. Work with parents and have honest discussions about whether a student has the ability to pass some school subjects.
4. Look carefully at interest areas of students. If a student desperately wants to become a vet but struggles with learning, maybe becoming a veterinary nurse or assistant is a good place to start.
5. Reassure students that they don't have to make big career decisions straight out of school. Our working lives are getting longer and longer so it is a good idea to find a career pathway that is of interest.

Case study – creating career options

Henry is one of the smartest people I have ever met. Henry won award after award at school and then moved to university to study Physiotherapy. At university, Henry again won award after award and upon completion of his studies, Henry was offered a job in a growing practice.

After three years of working in the practice, Henry was offered a partnership which he gratefully accepted. In order to do this, Henry took out a loan from the bank. Over the next five years Henry was married, bought a house, had children and was working hard to pay off his loans. The problem was, Henry began to hate his work as it was the same old, same old, every day of the week and this was required to pay his debts. Henry had trapped himself into a career that he didn't really like.

Fortunately for Henry, he was very smart and over two years, he completed studies in Business Administration. Through his studies, Henry was able to move away from practising as a physiotherapist to running and managing the practice.

The moral of the story is: don't get trapped into a career, give yourself options.

Counselling for career guidance 71

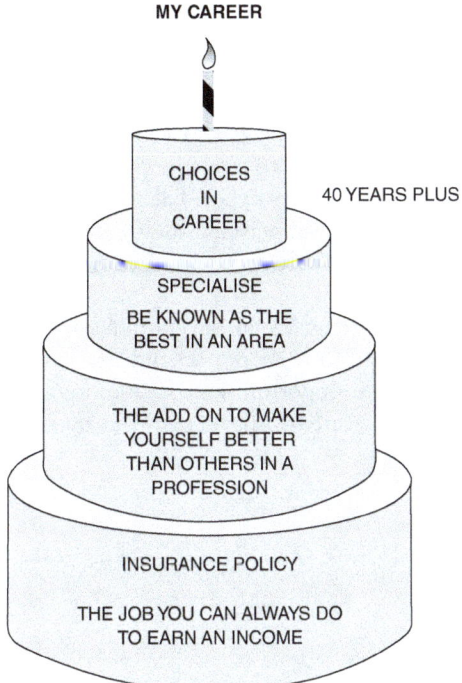

Figure 7 An example career cake

When doing career counselling with students I use the Career Wedding Cake – I ask students to look ahead into the future but most importantly to try to set themselves up with options.

The first step in the Career Wedding Cake is to help a student to identify the areas of interest for future work. This is not about being definite in a job but looking at what their interests are. Some areas of interest may be health, helping people, technology, being creative, science, practical work, the environment or business. Once this is established, the planning can begin.

Next we look to help the student to develop what I call the Insurance Policy. The Insurance Policy is a skill that will always assist in gaining some kind of employment. For many students this could be a part-time job, an apprenticeship or a university qualification. Ideally the Insurance Policy leads to full-time employment.

The next step is to make yourself better than everyone else – the reason why I say this is because the job market is a competitive place. I ask students "Why would I pick you for a job or even an interview?" "What is it that makes you stand out from the field?". This difference can be through volunteer work, previous part-time employment, having a second language, playing sport, travelling, playing music or doing a linked course of study.

Once in employment I encourage students to plan to make themselves the best in their field of work. This can be done through specialised training or even some diversification. For example, I have combined a degree in teaching with a degree in psychology, making me very specialised as there are not many people with this combination qualification. Make yourself the best in your field is what I encourage.

Finally, at age 40, I hope that students have choices – this means that a student can work in a variety of settings but can choose how much and what type of work they do.

The reason I adopt this theme with students is at age 40, you potentially have 30 years of working life ahead of you so it is important to keep building your career so that at age 40, you can have some choices in the type of work that you do.

There are many good career counselling online tools available to schools and I recommend that time is taken to find a programme that helps students to identify career interest areas to explore through work experience or career expos. I also believe it is the responsibility of the career counsellor to help a student understand their areas of interest and it is not to tell a student that a specific job is definitely for them. The student needs to decide this, not the person providing the guidance.

Career counselling is challenging, particularly when students have no idea about what it is that they want to do. This is okay and we need to reassure our students it is okay – always encourage students to keep learning, look for opportunities, ask questions of people in different vocations of interest and don't be scared to have a go, but please don't set students up to fail!

9 Counselling students who are developing an addiction to technology

It is clearly evident that technology is having a profound impact upon our students. Today's students have access to so much information at their fingertips through technology and devices (mobile phones and computers) – for many students, this is causing a problem as the dependence on technology is impacting upon their ability to function at school. We now have terms such as PMPU (problematic mobile phone use) and recently the condition of Internet Gaming Disorder has been added to the Diagnostic and Statistical Manual of Mental Disorders.

So, what can we do to help our students? The important thing is to try and understand the reasons as to why a student is so dependent on their device. Some of the possible reasons are:

- Depression.
- Anxiety.
- Deficits in social relationships.
- Shyness.
- Loneliness.
- Isolation.
- Impulsivity.
- Low self-esteem.
- Emotional difficulties.

For many students, technology fills a void or emptiness in their life. I hear of many students who feel comfortable talking to people online, but in real life they are very hesitant to engage in a conversation with a person they do not know. The interaction through games and chatting becomes a new world that is free from stress.

When students are spending too much time using technology the following symptoms can present at school:

- A lack of attendance.
- Fatigue (staying up at night, gaming or chatting).
- Decline in academic attainment.
- Withdrawal from social groups.
- Ceasing of physical activity such as sport.
- Looking pale and haggard due to not getting outdoors or not eating well.
- No future goals.

It is important that teachers and counsellors look for signs and talk to or refer on students who are showing any significant changes in their behaviours; it must be explored as to whether technology addiction is a factor.

Case study – computer addiction

Nick, a 16-year-old boy, presented as depressed; however, upon discussions with Nick it was learnt that he was spending a large amount of time on his computer at night, not sleeping, getting to school late, fighting with his parents and failing in his schooling. Nick's parents had given up fighting with him and were reluctant to make changes to the structure of the internet at home due to having other children.

Nick expressed that he had recently become very sad, describing how a friend of his had committed suicide. When asked about his friend Nick explained that he had never met the friend in real life, he had only been chatting to the person for the last three months. The person lived in Canada, was 24 years old and was addicted to heroin. The only time Nick could converse was at night due to Nick living in Australia and the time difference.

When talking further to Nick it was learnt that Nick had no real friendships at school. He had ceased playing all sport, socialising and his days at school were spent playing games on the computer at recess and lunchtimes. Nick was a student who described how when he was online playing games he could escape from the real world and people talked to him, showed him respect and listened to him. To Nick, the online world was much kinder that the current world he perceived. To Nick, his friend in Canada was a real friend and this was why he was so upset with his death.

Nick used the internet to escape as often as he could into the online world. Nick was addicted to technology as it met his social and emotional needs.

To help Nick we looked at the causes of his addiction. We addressed issues such as friendships, the stress of school work and overall health. This was done slowly and through the counselling process using the problem-solving model. Nick was also taught how to monitor his own use of technology, setting clear times for himself where he could spend time playing games and chatting to friends. The process was long, but over time Nick was able to re-establish some friendships and more importantly gain control over his addiction.

When first counselling students about technology I will ask questions like:

- Do you think you spend too much time on your phone or the computer?
- Has the time spent using technology impacted upon your friendships?
- Do your parents or friends comment about how much time you spend using technology?
- Does your time on technology stop you from doing other tasks?
- Have you tried to cut down your time?
- How much time is enough time using technology?
- When you are not using technology, what do you enjoy doing?

By gaining an understanding about the use of technology I can then work towards helping the student to create a balanced life of exercise, social time, study and using technology. Involving parents is also helpful as sometimes parents do have to exercise some tough love; without this, curbing the addiction can be hard. It never ceases to amaze me that parents will say that their children come back to them when away on holidays and there is no internet or Wi-Fi connection.

I recommend that the person working with the student gets support from teachers, who monitor closely what a student is doing in their lessons (learning not gaming) – also for some students, set homework tasks or work that does not need the internet. Too often students bluff parents with the old chestnut of "I need the internet to do my research and homework" when really the internet is to play games and chat to friends. Teachers can also help by monitoring school work closely and alerting parents when work is not being completed on time. Good communication can prevent an addiction at the early stages.

Counselling for technology addiction is not common in schools just yet but I think it will begin to occur more and more. If you are asked to counsel for technology addiction, I suggest you support the student by finding out the reason why they have become addicted then take the necessary steps to address the causes whilst helping the student to cut back their time and to develop a well-balanced lifestyle.

If a student is not making progress in controlling their addiction to technology and the signs associated with technology addiction are continuing, it is important professional support is gained. This is often completed through family therapy, as on most occasions parents need to make changes at home to their access to technology but need support whilst doing so. Together a family can establish rules to control an addiction whilst developing a balanced lifestyle.

10 Counselling for bullying

Unfortunately, bullying is something that is still occurring in our schools and despite many programmes aimed at intervention it appears that more and more students are reporting being bullied at some point throughout their education. As a result of this it is useful for counsellors within the school setting to have a plan/counselling procedure to follow when having to work with students who are being bullied or who are the bullies themselves.

I often ponder as to why bullying has not ceased in schools. At present many schools have implemented programmes such as Sticks and Stones, The Human Race, The Flipside and Cyberia; however, still bullying behaviours continue from some students. The website Stomp Out Bullying, (www.stompoutbullying.org) provides a very good resource as to why students bully others, as well as methods that are good to use to support students who are victims of bullying.

My thinking is that many students are exposed to bullying behaviours at home and then this becomes the norm. Students feel power through putting others down and it feels good, resulting in bullying behaviours. Some students are different in how they look, the things they like and how they behave and often this is not tolerated due to the role modelling provided at home.

We only have to look at how our politicians behave when in session and towards each other to see bullying behaviours. In sport, students are exposed to bullying behaviours, through the media and in some of the programmes they watch. As a result of all of this, bullying continues and this means schools and counsellors not only need to be prepared to support students, but also to work with the bullies to change their behaviours.

Case study – understanding bullying patterns in a school

A school counsellor had an unusual number of students who were reporting low level bullying behaviours amongst the Year 11 cohort of students (15 to 17 years old). To get a greater understanding of what was happening the school counsellor created a short survey for the students to complete, which was anonymous. There were three questions to the survey:

1. Who are the people who show good behaviours at school?
2. What are the main bullying behaviours that you see at school?
3. Who are the people who demonstrate bullying behaviours to their peers?

From this the counsellor was to ascertain which students were bullying others, but also in what shape or form. From here the counsellor created a list of the bullying behaviours which were written up onto a whiteboard. Behaviours such as name calling, hitting, pushing in lines, glaring, excluding, put downs, etc. were created into a list. The students whose names appeared a lot as people who demonstrated bullying behaviours were asked to come in and meet with the school counsellor. Once greetings were completed the counsellor asked the student to look at the list. The student was asked "Have you done any of these behaviours in the last two weeks at school?" The automatic reaction of many students was to deny but the counsellor then asked them to be honest, gave them a pen and asked them to put a tick next to any of the behaviours.

Once this was completed the counsellor explained to the student that their name had come up a lot as a student who was demonstrating bullying behaviours at school. Many students were mortified to think that they had been identified as a bully and were completely unaware of how their peers were perceiving them. The counsellor then asked the student "In ten years' time, when you attend a school reunion or bump into a peer who went to school with you, what will be their first memory of you?"

"Would you want the perception to be that you were a bully?"

Every student answered no, and the next question the counsellor asked was "So what do we now need to do to make the perception in ten years' time a good one?" Here the counselling/guidance began. The result of all of this was a significant reduction in bullying within the cohort.

This is just one example of how to tackle bullying and there are many approaches. The approach I first learnt when teaching, and the one I recommend today, is the method developed by Anatol Pikas in 2002 which is called "The Method of Shared Concern". The Pikas method has a success rate of approximately 80% – we must understand, counselling will not work with all bullies and when it does not work, consequences must be put into place. So how does the Pikas method work? I will run through a scenario to illustrate the process.

Scenario

Meeting 1 with Sam

Student 1, Sam (age 12) reports that Tom is bullying him in the classroom and in the yard. Sam has reported that Tom pokes him when sitting behind, calls him names when the teacher is not within hearing distance and pushes him around when lining up waiting for the teacher. Sam explained that he does not have a lot of friends and that Tom seems to be very popular, with many friends who laugh when he bullies Sam.

In this meeting with Sam I focus on the when, where and how, getting as much information as I can from Sam. The focus of the rest of the session is on helping Sam to develop some strategies to make sure he is safe, whilst also reassuring Sam that I will talk to his teacher so seating arrangements can be reviewed in the class. Line up procedures can also be reviewed. The initial plan is to help Sam to be safe, and in this case this can be done through teacher support.

Sam must be happy for action to proceed; on some occasions students do not want any action taken for fear of an increase in the bullying behaviours towards them.

Meeting 1 with Tom

Tom is somewhat bemused to be asked to meet with the school counsellor. The question asked to Tom is "Have you noticed any students who have been making life difficult for Sam at school?" Now Tom knows the counsellor is aware of his behaviours, but he has two obvious choices with his answer:

a)   Yes, I have seen some students be mean to him, or
b)   No, I haven't seen anything.

The response from the counsellor depends on the answer from Tom. If Tom answers a) Yes, I have seen Sam being given a hard time, the counsellor can ask Tom questions like:

- What do you think that must be like for Sam?
- Who are the students who you have seen give Sam a hard time?
- What do you think it would be like to be bullied?
- How do you think it feels to be bullied?
- Could you do anything to help Sam?

Hopefully through these questions Tom will understand that his behaviour towards Sam is impacting upon him and that Sam doesn't like it.

If Tom answers no, similar questions are asked with the final question being "If you saw Sam being bullied by students what would you do?" If Tom responded with nothing the counsellor response is "Well that is disappointing, but I really hope that you would not make things worse for Sam by joining in."

Tom leaves the counselling session knowing that his teachers are aware of his behaviours but somewhat happy that he is not in trouble or facing a consequence.

Meeting 2 with Sam

Hopefully Sam reports that things have improved and that Tom is leaving him alone. If this is the case, further work can be done with Sam to help him to build some coping skills for future use. Discussions can be had with Sam about what sort of behaviours may lead to bullying but most importantly how to keep himself safe.

Should Sam say that Tom has not ceased the behaviour, more information is gained as to the when, the where and the how. If possible, information can be gained from other students within the class as to what is happening. Teachers can complete surveys or questionnaires to gain information from students – or just a casual chat with some good, honest reliable students can get lots of information.

Ensuring Sam is safe is again the important role of the counsellor.

Meeting 2 with Tom

The tone of this meeting is somewhat different to the first meeting and the initial question is very direct. "Tom, I have been told that you have been bullying Sam, is this true?" Regardless of the response it is reinforced how hard this must be for Sam through conversation and Tom is specifically asked to leave Sam alone. Tom is also made aware that there would be consequences should the behaviours continue.

Part of the conversation with Tom should focus on the why – that is, why are you doing this to Sam? Is it to look cool, because Sam has done something to you, what is the reason? It may be that Tom needs some help to develop friendships or he has low levels of self-esteem and is putting Sam down to build himself up.

Case study – bullying behaviours

I met a student who was 14 years old and terrorised his peers through physical bullying. When talking to the student it was learnt that the student was treated this way at home and was powerless as his older brothers and father were brutal towards him. Being a bully at school was the only time the student had any power.

Meeting 3 with Sam

Check that the bullying behaviours from Tom have ceased, reinforce protective, resilience-building behaviours.

Meeting 3 with Tom

Praise Tom for leaving Sam alone and if necessary work further with Tom to help him to develop positive behaviours.

If behaviour has not ceased the meeting would be with a school leader who would look at consequences.

The aim of the method is for a bully to see how their behaviour impacts upon others, and in particular the target. It is hoped that the good nature of a person will take over and they will stop their behaviours. It also helps that there is no initial consequence, rather the behaviours are discussed first.

When counselling for bullying I encourage counsellors to look closely at the reasons why a student is being bullied. Often students are not aware of how their own behaviours impact upon others and how annoying the behaviours can be. Honest conversations have to be had at times. Another possible scenario is the idea that negative attention is better than no attention, resulting in some students behaving in a manner that attracts bullies.

Case study – social media and bullying

Marie, a 15-year-old girl, deliberately used social media to provoke responses from her peers. Marie would then go to the teacher and report bullying. It was only after some investigation that the teachers realised that it was in fact Marie who was making comments which were upsetting to people and after a while the people involved decided it was enough. Marie was then bombarded on social media and at school.

Through talking to Marie, the school counsellor identified that Marie was in fact quite lonely and lacking in the skills to build friendships. In time, Marie learnt some skills and was slowly able to build some friendships at school. An apology from Marie certainly helped.

Social media and bullying

So much bullying is done via social media and this is getting harder and harder for schools to monitor. My initial advice to students who are experiencing bullying via social media is to get off of it for a while, or at least agree not to chat or comment until what is happening can be explored with a counsellor. It is very useful for counsellors to have a good understanding of how social media works as well, so the advice given is accurate.

Many a student and parent have reported to me that most bullying stops when the use of social media stops. This is not rocket science! Parents can monitor the use and counsellors can teach coping skills and good communication skills. Too often parents have no idea about what their child is posting and the implications of the post. Vigilance across all social media is important when stopping bullying. The teaching of how to be a good friend can also never be underestimated.

Students must also be aware of the consequences associated with bullying through social media. Teaching students about how social media works and how what they post remains online forever, needs to be done.

Creating resilient bully-proof children

One of the challenges for schools is to help students to become resilient; in today's busy world it seems that resilience levels are dipping. One method I have used is to teach students to build their own levels of self-worth and self-esteem so when they are verbally bullied they have the thinking power and confidence to not let it affect them.

Case study – building bully-proof children

Hamish is a 9-year-old boy who has been verbally bullied by two of his classmates. The bullying is done in and outside of the classroom. Hamish is very short for his age, wears thick glasses, is not good at sport and is a very academic student. Hamish has a couple of friends who are similar to him in personality.

Hamish explained how he gets verbally bullied. I asked Hamish why he felt that the boys picked him to attack, to which he responded "I am small and not good at sport." I explored this further to discover that the bullies were very popular sporty kids. I then asked Hamish "What are you good at in school?" Hamish indicated that he was good at reading, spelling and maths but very good at computing. We explored this further to learn that the boys who were the verbal bullies were not good at these things.

I explained to Hamish that the boys who bully him are probably jealous of him because he is good at things when they are not, and what the boys were trying to do was to make him feel bad in order to make themselves feel good. They wanted to bring him down to bring themselves up. I drew three seesaws on the whiteboard.

Seesaw 1 is we are on equal terms.

Seesaw 2 is the bullies upsetting Hamish. The bullies are feeling good by making Hamish feeling bad.

Counselling for bullying 81

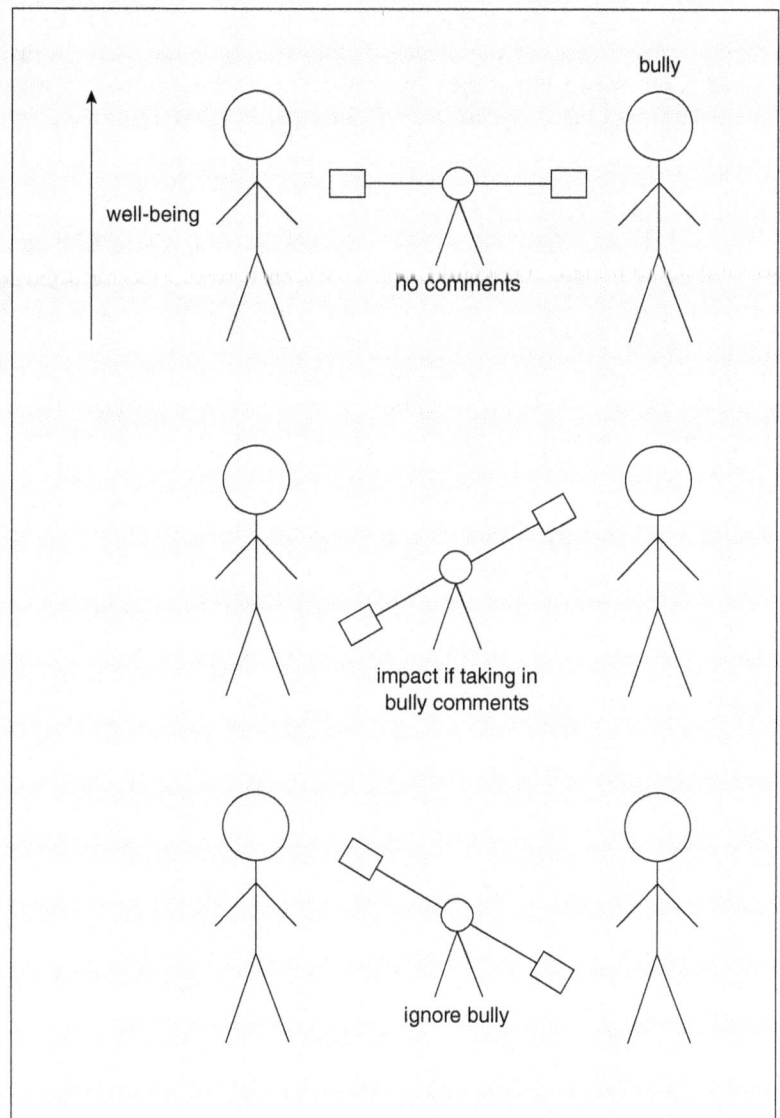

Figure 8 Reacting to bullying behaviours using a seesaw model

Seesaw 3 is Hamish feeling good knowing that the bullies attack him because they are feeling insecure about themselves and they want to bring Hamish down to make themselves feel good.

Hamish learnt that by not reacting and thinking to himself "The bullies attack me because I am better than them" that the bullies stopped, because they worked out that what they said did not bother Hamish in the slightest. We built Hamish's resilience through increasing his self-esteem and acknowledging his strengths whilst also giving him the skills of positive thinking.

I often teach kids who are being bullied to see it as a game. If you react, the bully wins as the bully feels better about themselves; if you don't react you win. I encourage students to keep a little score chart for themselves so they can show me their victories. What must be noted is that when physical bullying occurs the school must step in and have consequences – I am pleased to say that schools are becoming more and more proactive in doing this.

As I have said, unfortunately bullying has not stopped in school; however, working with students using the Pikas (No Blame Method) and creating resilient students are certainly good ways to help to reduce the amount of bullying within a school. I do say that the sooner the bullying behaviours of a person are addressed the better, and schools can be proactive in acting quickly to stop bullying whilst creating a positive and friendly environment for all students.

If a student is at a point where they are reluctant to go to school, external counselling is recommended. In this scenario a counsellor or health professional can work with a student on a very frequent basis to teach strategies whilst also working with the school and parents.

One of my personal favourite methods of helping students with bullying is to show them this video from YouTube: www.youtube.com/watch?v=7oKjW1OIjuw

Please watch this and have it up your sleeve as a resource.

11 Counselling for anger

I describe anger as a very powerful emotion that can easily get out of control, leading to very poor decisions being made. Students get angry through frustration, having feelings of being treated unfairly, not having things go as expected or being hurt. This becomes a problem when it interferes with a student's ability to function on a day-to-day basis within a school. What we can do is to help students to understand their anger and then introduce steps to prevent the triggers whilst at the same time introducing calming techniques for situations where anger feelings are increasing.

The first rule when counselling for anger is to not attempt any counselling when a student is angry; when a person is angry they do not listen, nor really have control of their emotions, so let the person calm down first. A common mistake many teachers make in classroom practice is to attempt to counsel or even talk to a student when they are in a fit of rage.

Where possible set up a safe place for a student to go so they can calm down. In the safe place I suggest that toys, activities, colouring in, etc. are ready so a student can walk in and get to these easily. For older students I sometimes use pillows so a student can grab a pillow and then shake it or squash it as a means of releasing anger. The other consideration is personal safety, as if a student is getting angry during counselling it may be of benefit to stop or to try a different tack. Our own safety is paramount when working with angry students – and also parents.

Once we have a student calmed down the key thing to do is to listen, but then to identify the cause. Often through listening and talking to a student we will identify the triggers and causes; once we have these, we can then set about teaching the student strategies to keep calm but also strategies to prevent the anger from escalating.

Case study – anger counselling

Ky is a 9-year-old boy who has recently moved to a new school as a result of being asked to leave his previous school due to his behaviours. On his first day in the new school Ky got angry in the yard and hit another student. When approached by the teacher, Ky became very angry, yelling and screaming at the teacher before climbing to the top of a tall tree on the school grounds. Fortunately, Ky was good at climbing so he was quite safe up in the tree but he would not come down for anyone.

(continued)

(continued)

When lunch finished and all of the attention had moved away from Ky as the students had gone back into class, Ky climbed down. When down, Ky's teacher asked him if he was ready to talk about what had happened to which Ky responded "No." The issue was not pushed and Ky and the teacher just sat before the teacher suggested that they go into the Sunshine Room (a room for counselling and sensory activities). Ky agreed to this.

Upon entering the Sunshine Room, Ky immediately went to the mini trampoline and started bouncing. After ten minutes Ky stopped and the teacher began talking to Ky. The conversation began by the teacher drawing a stick figure of Ky on the whiteboard and the teacher asking Ky to tell him about himself, what he liked, what his previous school was like. Slowly Ky opened up.

Once the teacher had learnt a little about Ky the teacher wrote the word *Anger* in red next to the stick figure of Ky and he said "Ky, anger is one of your behaviours but what I want you to do now is to tell me about some of your good behaviours that you can show." With some prompting, Ky revealed that he was caring (dog and younger brother), funny, good at sport, good at Lego, good at bike riding, loving of his family and kind to his friends. All of these were written in blue.

The next step was to talk about the not good behaviours such as anger and again with prompting Ky indicated that he got angry quickly, hit others when angry, yelled at people, didn't do what he was told and ran away. These were written in red.

The next step was to reinforce to Ky that he did in fact have many good qualities and behaviours in him and he was encouraged to demonstrate some of the behaviours at home after school. With the "not good" behaviours Ky was asked what he could do to reduce these behaviours and the solution process began. Together Ky and the teacher worked on some solutions, one of which was Ky would rate how he was feeling in the morning upon arriving to school so adjustments could be made to his learning if he was uptight, and that Ky would go straight to the Sunshine Room if he was feeling angry at any time. Over time, Ky settled. Ky's progress was also helped by teachers being aware of his triggers and picking appropriate battles whilst also giving Ky lots of positive comments and acknowledgement of good behaviour.

Ky's example is just one method that I think works well when counselling for anger. I try to get students to understand that anger is a powerful emotion that we need to learn to control but it is just one of our many emotions. I also encourage teachers to help students to learn to use their anger for good. An example of this has been when I have suggested to students they target their anger at a ball in sport or when tackling in games. Anger creates great energy and this can be harnessed in sport.

Setting up a safe spot for students to go when angry can prevent many situations from escalating. A student could be given a card and when required, the student can show to card to the teacher. This then leads to the student going to a quiet place to calm down, but to also talk about why they have chosen to use the card. Students can't simply have a card to get them out of class without having to explain the reason why.

I have also noticed a lot of student anger occurs in the yard when play is unsupervised. As a school this is an issue that can be discussed so solutions can be developed. Learning the rules of games and sticking to them helps, as many boys fight over rules leading to anger outbursts. Using older students as mentors can also help in the yard.

When counselling for anger, the Solution-Focused Counselling Model works very well, but what needs to be established is what it is that makes a student angry – when we understand the triggers we can modify. Here are some things that can make students angry:

- Being picked on by other students.
- Being picked on by teachers.
- Not being listened to.
- Being embarrassed in class or by peers.
- Not knowing how to do school work.
- Being told off or kept in for not doing work.
- Not getting enough sleep – many students have meltdowns when they are tired.
- Not eating enough.
- Unsettling home life.
- Having anger role modelled at home as a way to solve things.

As I have said, find the cause of the anger and then work towards the solution but always remember not to attempt any counselling until the student has calmed down. If necessary, this can be done the next day. I must also stress that the relationship between the teacher and the angry student is important, because if a student likes the teacher the anger level will decrease very quickly. Building relationships is very important in having a happy school yard.

Case study – school yard anger

A school was having difficulty with the students arguing and fighting during play times; thus a solution was needed as the following learning time was being taken up by sorting out play time squabbles. The teachers decided firstly to go out and play in the yard with students every Friday for 15 minutes. The students loved this, as did many of the teachers. Secondly the play time was extended by 15 minutes on the Friday if there were no more than ten reports of poor play time behaviours. In order to achieve this, the teachers worked with their classes on rules, behaviours and how to sort out difficulties. Again, over time the behaviours improved and the teacher–student relationships were enriched by playing together.

Never be scared to try different techniques for counselling for anger whilst knowing that the Solution-Focused Counselling Model is a good base.

12 Counselling for anxiety

It has certainly become apparent to me in my practice that more and more students are presenting with and displaying signs and symptoms associated with anxiety. Given this, it goes without saying that within schools, more and more students are doing the same; that is, arriving each day at school with some form of anxiety – albeit mild to severe. As a result of this, it is imperative that today's teachers have knowledge of what anxiety is, but also what they can do within a counselling role to help the anxious student.

So, what is anxiety?

I define anxiety in the following way: *Anxiety is a condition where a student has excessive worry that they can't control, which then impacts upon their ability to function to their full capacity.*

Within the broader term of anxiety there are a number of types, some of which can impact upon a student's well-being. But before exploring this I always think about what the possible causes of anxiety are for students. Here is a list of what I believe to be some of the causes:

- The pressure of completing exams/tests.
- Making and maintaining friendships.
- Attending certain classes.
- Teachers and how teachers interact with a student.
- The required school work.
- A student's home life.
- Anxious role models (parents).
- Pressure to succeed at sport, music, drama, etc.
- Moving to a new school.
- Getting lost at school.
- Public speaking.
- Parents separating.
- Entering into a relationship.
- Breaking up from a relationship.
- Going to a school formal.
- Asking a date to a formal.
- Fear of being judged by peers on looks/possessions.
- Being asked questions in a lesson.
- Body image.
- Posting on social media.

- Feeling left out.
- Not being picked up after school.
- Fearing something will happen to loved ones whilst at school.

This is just a small sample of some of the things that can lead to student anxiety; as teachers it is good to know the signs and symptoms so we can initiate conversations to help anxious students. So what are the signs and symptoms of anxiety? Many students will show the following behaviours:

- Seek reassurance or often avoid situations they feel worried or scared about.
- Try to get others to do the things they are worried about.
- Tell you they have physical pains.
- Dislike taking risks or trying new things.
- Have lots of fears.
- Get upset easily.
- Have lots of worries.
- Ask for help with things they can do for themselves.
- Worry a lot about doing things right.
- Prefer to watch others rather than have a go.
- Scared of the dark, dogs, injections, being alone, germs, tests.
- Often cry over small things.
- Complain about being picked on a lot.
- Always see the dangerous or negative side of things.
- Write negative thoughts or draw negative pictures.

When teachers notice a student is displaying signs of anxiety it is important to act quickly and have a chat to the student to prevent the anxiety level escalating. Within the conversation the causes of the anxiety can be established, which then leads to action being taken to reduce it.

Case study – helping with anxiety

It was noticed by a teacher that 13-year-old Kym had started to withdraw from his friendships, choosing to spend more and more time by himself. Kym's parents, who were concerned about Kym's withdrawal from friends at home, explained that Kym was moving interstate to a new school at the end of the year. As a result of this, Kym's teacher organised a time to sit down and have a chat to Kym about what was happening and how he was feeling.

In the discussions Kym indicated that he was feeling scared about the future. He had thoroughly enjoyed his time at school with his friends and he was very sad and scared that he would be leaving. To help Kym his teacher did the following:

1. Worked with Kym on ways to keep contact with his friends (social media).
2. Ensured Kym had good skills in making and keeping friendships (reinforced Kym's skills he already had).

(continued)

(continued)

3 Looked at planning Kym's participation in the end-of-year arrangements and worked with Kym in planning a strategy to make sure he enjoyed himself (positive thinking and positive self-talk).
4 Helped Kym to learn about his new school and what it offered to help Kym to build new friendships.

Through this, Kym's anxiety reduced significantly. What was needed was some planning and processes to help Kym. Through having some simple things in place Kym felt more in control, thereby reducing his anxiety.

I must point out that some anxiety is normal and a lack of some anxiety can lead to a lack of safety or an over confidence, which can end badly. A lack of preparation for an exam due to feeling over confident is an example of this. So, when is anxiety not normal? My idea is that when anxiety stops a person from functioning to the level that they want to, it is a problem and needs to be addressed. An example of this may be when a student is unable to enter a classroom for fear of what the teacher may say, or a student is unable to go into a cafeteria due to fear of what a person may think. In these cases, a student is not able to function and do the things they want to do. When this is happening, we can help our students through using some of the following techniques.

Techniques for counselling for anxiety

The following are some of the techniques I use for counselling anxious students.

Thought blocking

Often, anxious students will talk about their thoughts spiralling out of control and as a result they become more and more anxious.

Failing exam example

In the example the negative thought is blocked and then challenged (left-hand side of Figure 9). To help students block the thought they could use a visual cue as a reminder, such as a sticky note on a wall. Another tool might be wearing a rubber band on the wrist which can be flicked when an anxious thought happens, as a reminder to block the thought. Wearing a piece of clothing or jewellery can also be used. The key is to find a way to block the initial negative thought which is replaced with the neutral or positive thought.

Writing this process of thinking up on a whiteboard also allows a student to see their thoughts and helps in teaching them how to write down what they are thinking, leading to a restructuring of thoughts.

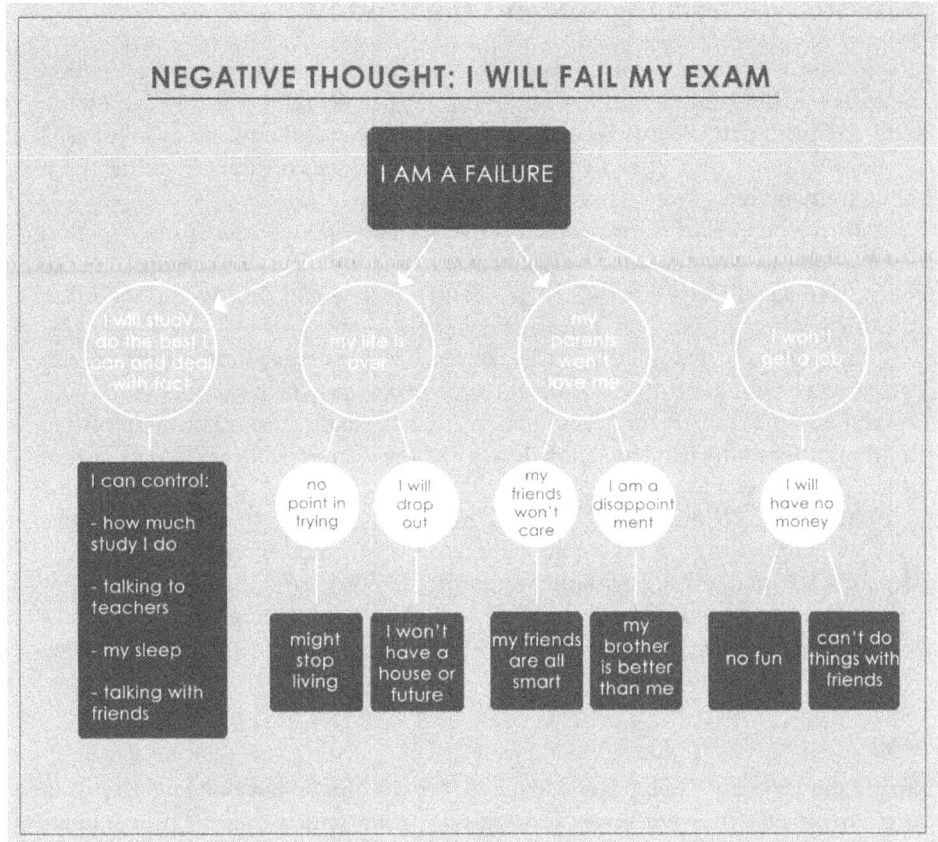

Figure 9 Anxiety thought blocking process

Deal with fact (DWF)

As mentioned in Chapter 5, DWF is the process of teaching a student to only deal with facts and not *what could*, *what might* or *what if*. The process involves asking a student to identify thoughts that are worry thoughts. A student is then asked to identify the thoughts which are actually real events or facts that have happened. The focus is to help a student to learn to only concern themselves with things that have actually happened – facts – whilst looking at ways to reduce the worries. In teaching a student DWF we also ask the student to identify a support network for when a fact occurs. With the aid of the support network, the fact is dealt with through counselling.

I was told once that 99% of the things we worry about never happen. DWF is a good way to teach kids to worry less. I often use DWF with younger students who have separation anxiety at school or for older students who are worried about exams or career pathways.

DWF can also be reinforced by visual cues. Having DWF written on a sticky note stuck to a bathroom mirror or on the fridge can remind students to apply the idea; that is, things should be dealt with when they happen.

Case study – teaching students how to DWF

12-year-old Carly is particularly worried that she will be left out of a friendship group as this has happened to her in the past. When working with the counsellor Carly indicated that she worries excessively about her friendships and as a result she is constantly trying to be friendly to everyone meaning she is drifting from friendship group to friendship group.

With the counsellor Carly worked through the friendship model (see Figure 6 on page 66) to establish who she would really like to be friends with. From here the counsellor helped Carly to DWF. This meant Carly would only worry about her friendships when she got cues that may suggest a concern. The established cues were body language, not being included in conversations at recess and lunchtimes, not being invited with the group to weekend activities and generally being left out. Carly was also taught not to overreact as sometimes friends can be short in conversation due to having a lot on their minds. Carly learnt that the changes in behaviour by friends needed to be over a few days.

If there were changes to the behaviours of friends Carly would recognise this as a fact and then together the counsellor and Carly would work through it. The idea for Carly being that you should not worry about what if, or what might, but rather have the support networks in place to deal with something when it happens.

Scaling

Scaling is the process of helping a student to identify the severity or intensity of their feelings. Items of worry are given a rating on a scale which then helps a student to gain perspective on the intensity of their worry. It is a very good teaching technique

Worry/Anxiety

5		freaking out panic
4		really worried
3		worried nervous anxious
2		a little worried
1		okay

Figure 10 Anxiety level/Worry scale

as students can learn very quickly how to rate any event that happens to them or thought they experience before working through strategies to help. Scaling works very well when working with anxiety as it allows students to rate how much the worry is impacting upon them. For younger students visual scales can be used such as the one in Figure 10.

Using the scale students can see that the worry they have need not to be such a worry. Strategies are then introduced to help to reduce the worry. Sometimes helping a student to gain some perspective can make a lot of difference.

Can control vs. can't control

A technique for older students is Can control vs. can't control. Students are asked to write down all of the things that are worrying them and they are then asked to write either *can control* or *can't control* next to the worry; *can control* is a worry they can exert influence over, whereas *can't control* is a worry they have no control over. Again, a whiteboard is very helpful when doing this exercise.

Case study – Can control vs. can't control

17-year-old Simon is worried about failing his final year exams. When asked to write the can control vs. can't control, Simon created the following list:

Can control	*Can't control*
How much study I do	The questions in the exam
How much sleep I have	How my answers are interpreted
My communication with teachers	The weather on the day
How much I go out before exams	Unexpected tragedy
My pre-exam preparation	Getting hurt playing sport
How much exercise I do	Needy friends
How much time I spend on the computer	Noisy siblings
Social media use	Parent demands
My time uses	
Being on time to the exam	
Getting accustomed to the exam room	
My equipment for exams	
The place I study	

After creating the list, the counsellor and Simon worked through the Can control list establishing clear plans of how Simon could ensure control of the items. For example, Simon decided that he would socialise with his friends on Saturday nights only until after the exams. On Friday nights Simon decided that he would play computer games. Together the counsellor and Simon created a plan to keep as many things in control as possible.

For the Can't control list, Simon was taught DWF knowing that he was supported should something from the list occur. By gaining control of things, Simon's worries decreased.

Can control vs. can't control is a good way of helping a student to wrestle control of their worries. An important point that goes with this, is that students must be prepared to put the work in to keep control. In Simon's case he would soon lose control and worry more if he did not do enough study.

When working with students I often remind them of this: "Learning to control anxiety is like the learning of any new skill; that is, you have to practise it and keep practising it because if you stop practising you will lose your skill." Visual cues, positive notes, timetables, etc. are all helpful to support anxious students.

Worry time

Worry time is a technique that works well with Can control vs. can't control. It is giving students the opportunity to set aside some time to worry, whilst also working through the exercise of Can control vs. can't control. In Worry time, students set aside some time during the day to work through all of the things they are worried about. This may be at a set time and for 30 minutes. At the conclusion of Worry time, the student then does something which has been identified as a happy activity, such as exercise, playing music or watching a favourite TV programme.

Free writing can also be used in Worry time and this is where students can write all of the thoughts that are in their head. I find that by asking students to do this we can then start to talk through some of the worries. Alternatively, it can help a student to clear their thoughts before going to sleep.

When it all gets too much – professional help

Unfortunately, for many students their levels of anxiety reach such heights that they are unable to function and in some cases, attend school. When this does occur, it is important that students are guided to professional help, whether that be to a doctor or mental health professional. If this does occur it is important that the school works closely with the health professional to best support the student.

When working with a student who is seeing an external health professional, the best thing to do is to let the student know that you as a counsellor are there to help them wherever possible within the school environment. A common question that can be asked of students is "If there is anything I can do to help you at school, please let me know?" More often than not, the student knowing that the school is supporting them helps greatly.

Communicating with the teachers of a student also makes a difference, as then all of the teachers know the situation. To sit with a student and send a group email to all teachers allows the student to feel safer in classes whilst knowing that the teachers know and understand the current situation.

An email to teachers may read as follows.

To all teachers of James Krieg. Please be advised that James is experiencing difficulty in attending some classes and completing school work at present. James is receiving support through an external psychologist but I would ask that you monitor James's progress in your class and advise me of any concerns you have regarding James.
 Thanks
 Tim

At the same time, if you are working with a student and you feel that the student is not making any progress a referral to an external professional is in order. As mentioned previously, a good network of allied health professionals is an important tool for any counsellor within a school. An option for schools is to contact a local medical clinic that has general practice doctors, but also a wide range of other allied health professionals such as speech pathologists, psychologists and occupational therapists, and then work towards developing an ongoing working relationship between the school and the practice.

Teaching of anxiety skills and practice

Like all skills, anxiety training needs to be practised. Setting little practice exercises for students helps, whilst monitoring learnt skills. There are many good referral sources for students online at present that students and teachers can access to develop skills. One of my favourite resource tools is Mood Gym (https://moodgym.com.au).

The Mood Gym workbook can be purchased by schools and teachers can be trained in how to use the programme; what I like about the programme is that students can go back to the course at any time to refresh their skills.

There are also many tools available either online or as mobile phone applications. My suggestion is to take the time to look at a small number that are specific to anxiety, learn how to use them and then recommend them to students. Having self-help tools that can be accessed at any time is reassuring for many students. Some apps that have been reviewed and recommended by the Anxiety and Depression Association of America are:

- Headspace
- Anxiety Reliever
- Anxiety Coach
- Breathe to Relax

A personal favourite of mine is The Mindfulness App. All of the apps mentioned can be found through searching for the name of the app + *Anxiety* on the internet.

Anxiety is a normal part of everyday life, so the best thing we can do as teachers/counsellors is to give our students the skills to be able to face their fears or challenges with tools that they can use, whilst reassuring them that we are there to help should the need apply. The website Beyond Blue (www.beyondblue.org.au) provides a wonderful resource for teachers and students to learn about anxiety and, importantly, what students can do to help themselves to manage their anxiety.

13 Counselling for depression

As indicated in Mission Australia's 2016 Youth Survey Report, many more students are presenting with the signs and symptoms of depression. Just like anxiety it is very important for any counsellor who is working with a student who is showing the signs and symptoms of depression to seek professional support and to work with the support to care for the student. With this is mind there are still many things counsellors within a school can do when working with a student.

What is depression?

When running Basic Counselling Skills for Teachers I always ask the group this question: "What is depression?". The most common responses are:

- Intense feelings of sadness.
- Not having motivation to do things that were previously enjoyable.
- Grades at school dropping.
- Withdrawing from social events.
- Spending a lot of time in bedroom but not doing much.
- Having lots of negative self thoughts.
- Thoughts of self harm.
- Feeling tired a lot and sleeping a lot.
- Feeling sick a lot of the time.

All of these are symptoms of depression. My own definition is: *Depression is having intense feelings of sadness, a lack of motivation and not wanting to do things that were once enjoyed for an extended period of time.* I deliberately keep this definition simple so it easy to understand for students. I also use the Beyond Blue website (www.beyondblue.org.au) to help students understand clearly what depression is, the signs and symptoms, the causes – but most importantly what the best treatment plan is.

A part of counselling as a teacher is to try and understand how a student is feeling so empathy can be shown. In order to do so I believe it is important to have some understanding of what a condition is. With depression, information can be gained via websites such as Beyond Blue or the Black Dog Institute, (www.blackdoginstitute.org.au). Being able to access information and learning about depression helps us to understand what a student may be experiencing.

A challenge faced by many counsellors in schools is when students present who have self-diagnosed and state they are depressed. Having knowledge about depression allows a counsellor to ask the right questions to try and find out what has caused the student to feel as they do. It is also important that we educate students about depression. Too often students will use the term *depression* to describe how they are feeling as a result of an event: "I have double Maths today, it is so depressing." Another example is "I am depressed, as I can't go to the concert." Some teaching here for students is a good idea.

One of the challenges, as I have said, is when students self-diagnose. Unfortunately, there are so many online checklists that students can complete – often the resulting diagnosis is based on an event or series of events that has led a student to feel very poorly. With careful questioning we can establish how severe the feelings are and then determine if a referral to a professional is warranted.

Case study – situational depression

15-year-old Willow in Year 11 at school sits down and states that she is depressed. Willow has completed an online questionnaire with her results indicating that she has moderate depression. When asked what her symptoms are Willow explained that she is very tired, sleeps all of the time, lacks motivation to study or complete homework and she finds it hard to concentrate.

When asked about friendships Willow explained that she has great friends and that the only time she was happy was on the weekends when she was able to spend time with her friends, going to parties and socialising. With further questioning, Willow explained that she had recently been fighting with her parents, who had taken her computer privileges away and who were now monitoring her social media access.

What became apparent was that Willow certainly had symptoms of depression; however, the symptoms occurred between 8.45am and 3.15pm from Monday to Friday but when Willow was away from school, with her friends and doing what she wanted to do she was happy. The process for Willow was to work through how the pressure of school could be reduced whilst we looked at ways to help Willow to rebuild the relationship with her parents. At the same time, Willow also needed to be educated as to what depression was.

Willow had what I describe as situational depression, which was caused by school, her parents and not getting what she wanted. Sadly, I have seen situations where students have gone directly to doctors who immediately prescribe medication – as a result of the confirmation of a diagnosis of depression, parents back off and allow students to do what they want with the parents thinking that in allowing this, the child will be happy. The website for Mental Health America, (www.mentalhealthamerica.net/stressed-or-depressed-know-difference) provides excellent information for parents and students in how to identify the differences between stress and depression, whilst the website for Healthline, (www.healthline.com/health/depression/depression-vs-sadness) provides excellent information on the difference between sadness and depression. Again, another good resource for students, parents and teachers.

Often in my practice I ask parents to see how a student who is showing signs of depression behaves in the holidays. More often than not parents report back that the student is happier and a lot more relaxed. Too often it is the pressure and stress of school that causes the symptoms of depression.

Within a school we need to know the signs and symptoms but also be confident enough to talk to a student and ask questions relating to the condition. The types of questions I encourage a counsellor to ask are:

- How long have you been feeling this way?
- Have you felt like hurting yourself?
- Have you had thoughts of killing yourself? (We need to ask the safety questions.)
- Do your parents know how you are feeling?
- Do your friends know how you are feeling?
- Has anything changed recently in your life?
- How is school going? (Ask about marks, study, exams, etc.)
- Do you have some good friends?
- Are you spending time with your friends?
- How much sleep are you getting at night?
- What time are you going to bed?
- Are you eating well?
- Are you doing any exercise?
- Are there any times when you are feeling happy?
- Would you like to talk to a doctor about how you are feeling?

By asking questions like these we can get an idea of how a student is going but also the severity of the depression. Based on the answers we can then decide the best course of action. Using scaling questions can also help to get an idea of how a student is feeling. If in doubt I recommend that we talk to the external professionals and/or parents to get advice on the best treatment pathway.

One of the most important questions we can ask a student is "How can I help you?" whilst also reassuring the student that you are there to help and support them. Making a follow-up appointment is a good idea as it allows further discussions but also a chance to monitor progress and how a student is feeling.

Knowing what to look for in a depressed student is useful for counsellors and teachers. I cannot stress enough how important the communication between teachers and the school counsellor is when a student is showing behaviours that are of concern.

Students with depression may display these symptoms:

- Depressed or irritable mood.
- Difficulty sleeping or concentrating.
- Change in grades, getting into trouble at school or refusing to go to school.
- Change in eating habits.
- Feeling angry or irritable.
- Mood swings.
- Feeling worthless or restless.
- Frequent sadness or crying.

- Withdrawing from friends and activities.
- Loss of energy.
- Low self-esteem.
- Thoughts of death or suicide.

If some or all of these behaviours have been observed it is important to act and check how a student is going.

Counselling the depressed student

In a perfect world a student who has been diagnosed as having depression is receiving help from a psychologist or counsellor and the external professional is feeding back information so that the student can be further supported at school. As I have mentioned, one of the best things a school counsellor can do is to work with the student to establish what can be done within the school setting to help. This might be in the form of communicating with teachers, assisting in the modification of the curriculum and giving the student a safe place to go and sit/talk whenever needed.

As a part of counselling in a school, strategy can also be taught to help a student. In the very beginning of the book I talked about how sometimes a student will choose you as the person to provide counselling and if this occurs it is good to know how to help. Some of the strategies I use in counselling for depression are:

1 Use the five secrets of happiness and ask the student to try and implement all of the secrets each week. The secrets are Give, Learn, Exercise, Take Notice and Spend Time with Positive People. In counselling, a student can talk about how they have applied the secrets. An explanation of the areas is provided in Chapter 14, "Looking after yourself".
2 Use goal setting to work towards improving sleep, diet, exercise, etc.
3 Focus on the future. Talk about the good things that are ahead and plan for them.
4 Introduce positive thinking processes and thought blocking techniques.
5 Have a homework book to record thoughts and feelings that can be monitored.
6 Establish things that help to change moods, such as television programmes or music.

More often than not I use a combination of techniques, based on the needs of the student and the information provided. I do find that removing stress is a very good start and if school is a cause of stress this needs to be explored and methods established to remove it. This can be difficult, as modifying the curriculum and not completing work can make passing a year challenging; however, a person's mental health is much more important and this should never be forgotten. Study can be caught up when a student is well.

I believe that counselling a student who has been diagnosed with depression is very much a team effort with external professionals, parents, teachers and the school counsellor all involved. It takes time, patience and good communication between all of the parties involved. When this occurs, students can be supported and learn skills to help themselves feel better, thus reducing – and in many cases removing – their symptoms.

Practising your skills

Something we must all do is to practise our skills. I don't ever finish a counselling session and then have a student say "Tim, I liked your relaxed approach and your open questions; however, I don't think you clarified my concerns very well." The fact is, we never really know how we are going unless we practise and have people observe us whilst we work.

In a school setting it is not always possible to have people watch and observe you; however, where possible I recommend that you attend counselling training courses or watch YouTube clips so you can see how other people work or learn new skills. The best counselling training courses will teach you some new skills or techniques whilst having you work in a small group so you can get feedback on your counselling techniques.

Aim to do some practice every year with feedback given. It helps to keep your skills sharp.

14 Looking after yourself when counselling

A very common question I am asked is "How do you do what you do?"; that is, listen to and work at trying to help people of all ages, all day. Upon reflection, this is a very good question and one that does need exploring. I have always promoted the mantra of "If you do not look after yourself, how can you look after others?" To me, this is important in counselling as we need to ensure we are in a good headspace so we can really focus on the clients we are working with. To stay in a good headspace, I try and follow/practise the following five things.

1   Exercise – regular exercise allows the opportunity to clear your head and think things through. I understand that we are not all elite athletes but time spent walking, gardening, doing yoga, tai chi, etc. are all important to our overall well-being. Exercising also releases endorphins, the body's natural feel good chemical.
2   Learn – too often people forget about learning for their own interest rather than purely for professional interest/requirement. Learning keeps our brains active and it often invokes passion on a topic. I encourage people to learn in a wide range of topics such as cooking, gardening, a second language, a musical interest, a recreational activity such as yoga, reading on a topic of interest, etc. Learning is a means of unwinding and taking our minds away from our day-to-day stress.
3   Give – do the little things for others without asking anything of anyone else. Within a school setting this can be supporting colleagues, celebrating birthdays or being a part of a morning tea/soup roster. It can also be getting involved in an external charity or community where support and help is needed. Giving makes us feel good.
4   Surround yourself with positive people – unfortunately within life we all encounter the dementors, the people who just seem to suck the life out of others. The positive people can be within or outside of school, but we all need people who make us laugh and have fun. Positive people give us positive energy to keep going and doing what we are doing in helping others.
5   Take notice – stop and smell the roses. Looking after yourself involves keeping a good perspective on life and in order to do so it is important to stop and appreciate things, events, the people around you and the small things that happen during the day. Practising mindfulness allows us to become more aware of what is happening in our day and stopping to take notice of the good things helps us to be happy.

I am a strong believer in the fact that if you do not look after yourself, you cannot look after others. As teachers or counsellors, it is important to be aware of our own well-being and to ensure we are taking steps to enhance it on a daily basis.

Another practice that helps when looking after yourself is to simply work through the Solution-Focused Counselling Model using your own stress as the issue. It is amazing how we can solve so many stressors just by working through this model. Talking to a trusted colleague on a regular basis is also a good idea.

So, how do we know we are getting burnt out?

The first thing is, counsellors need to be able to identify the signs of stress/work burn out. The following are typical signs of teacher stress:

- Being under constant pressure to meet with students within a limited set time.
- Work requiring lots of energy over a long time and after hours.
- A lack of trust between individuals and others.
- Working under difficult circumstances with difficult groups.
- Having unresolved personal conflicts.
- Inadequate training for the task.
- Insufficient resources.
- Insufficient time.
- No support or encouragement from colleagues or management.
- Being subjected to criticism, humiliation, bullying at work.
- No relaxation.
- Personal needs not being met.
- Giving large amounts of personal and emotional energy to others without results.

How many signs do you identify with?

Once we have identified that we are experiencing stress, the next stage is to put strategies in place that help us to reduce it and become proactive in caring for ourselves and that present stress – a key factor in this is Principal and colleague support. The hardest step is to identify there *is* stress and then to take action – but remember, if we don't look after ourselves we can't properly look after others.

Find groups of people – preferably fellow school counsellors or people in a similar role to you at your school and other schools – and arrange regular catch-ups and professional development together.

Look after yourself and care for your colleagues.

Conclusion

Thank you for taking the time to read this book and I wish you well in counselling students. One of my greatest memories was when I was sitting quietly watching a game of basketball at a stadium and a young man with a baby came up and said "Hello, Mr Dansie." A conversation began and the young man explained how when he was in Year 10, twelve years ago, he visited my office on three occasions and I listened to him and helped him. The young man said how he wished he had thanked me at the time but he did not have the maturity to do so, but he was very grateful for the time we spent talking.

You see, sometimes it does not feel like you are making a difference, when by just being there, listening and showing you care makes all of the difference to a student.

Best wishes in your counselling and keep making a difference.

Cheers,

Tim

Please feel free to contact me at tdpsych@bigpond.com as I am always willing to visit schools and work with staff, students and parents. I also run seminars on counselling skills for staff.

Appendix

Tools to help students to talk

Use a genogram

A genogram is a way for us to gain an understanding of a student's family structure. This can be very helpful in allowing us to understand why a student may behave as they do, but also some of the challenges they may face on a day-to-day basis. It is also a very good way of getting a student to open up and talk.

The genogram uses symbols to represent family members. Here are some examples.

Square (males), circle (females), a line with a cross through it means the couple, have separated, a symbol with a cross through it means a person has died. I have always encouraged teachers to be creative when doing genograms with students by adding pets (triangles), adding the ages and names of people and including grandparents and some other relatives who are in the student's life. The aim of a genogram is to learn about a student.

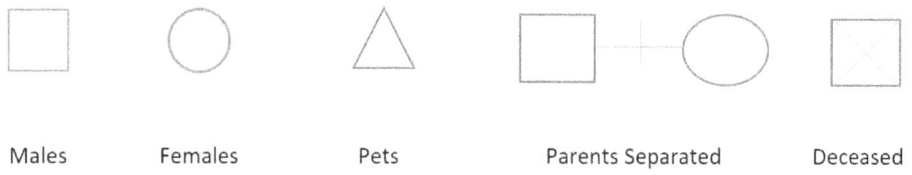

Males   Females   Pets   Parents Separated   Deceased

Figure 11 Genogram symbols to use with students

Case study – a genogram

Paul is 8 years old and new to the current school. Very little information has been included in Paul's file and his mother has not been at all forthcoming in providing a background about Paul's previous education. What is known is that Paul has attended five different schools in his three years of education and that he has an elder brother and younger sister. Paul has displayed attention-seeking behaviours, he is often tired, he is below the class level in numeracy and literacy, but at times he shows a very good understanding of learning and social awareness.

(continued)

(continued)

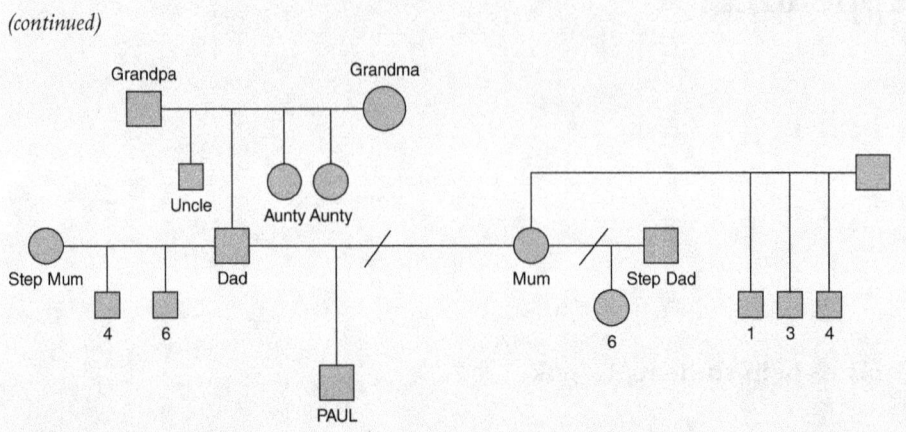

Figure 12 Example of a genogram

From the genogram it can be seen that Paul's mother and father have separated with Paul's father remarrying a partner who has two other children. Paul's mother has remarried and separated having had Paul's younger sister with her second husband and she now has a new partner, who Paul and his siblings live with. Paul's mother's partner has three children from previous relationships. It is evident that Paul's grandparents are alive and that he has an uncle and two aunties.

Whilst creating the genogram the teacher asked Paul the questions below – it is through the construction of the genogram that the information about Paul is gained. Paul was always asked to provide names and he was asked questions about his relationships with the key people in the genogram. Paul was encouraged to talk about his relationships with the people in the genogram but also what life was like living in his current arrangement.

- How many people are in your family?
- Are your mum and dad still married and living together?
- Has you mum or dad remarried?
- Are your mum and dad still with their partners?
- Has your mum got a new partner?
- Do you have any brothers or sisters?
- Do you have any step brothers or sisters?
- Are your grandparents alive?
- Do you have any aunties or uncles?
- Do you live at your father's house as well as your mother's house?
- Is it very crowded in your mother's house?
- What days do you spend with your father?
- Are there different rules at your father's house compared to your mother's house?

What was learnt about Paul was that he desperately missed his father, and in particular the times on weekends where he would play with his dad. Paul's father was a fly-in, fly-out worker in the mining industry, meaning that he would be home one week in four. It was also learnt that Paul did not like his mother's new partner and at his mother's house there was very little for him to do, due to the house being very small and having a lot of people in it. Paul was sharing a bedroom at his mother's house but at his father's place he had his own room.

Paul also missed the contact of his grandparents (father's side) and he found it very hard to make friends at school because he feared that his mother would move again meaning that Paul would change schools again. Paul described how hard he found parts of literacy and numeracy as he had moved schools a number of times and in the process missed large chunks of school due to not going at all. Paul did not attend kindergarten as his parents separated when he was aged 4 and about to attend.

Paul's behaviour was attributed to the events of his childhood and the implication of his parent's separation on his education, social development and overall levels of well-being. Paul's teacher described how through talking, Paul opened up and strategies were developed to help him to settle into the classroom and daily routines of school. Social skills training was provided and Paul was given lots of positive reinforcement for good behaviours. Unfortunately, Paul moved school again six months later due to his mother's relationship breaking down.

A genogram is a good way of getting to know a student and then using the information to work out why they may behave as they do. It also allows for a good relationship to develop between the teacher and student due to the opportunity for a one-to-one chat.

Helping younger students to talk

Help younger students to talk by saying a word and asking the student to point to the face that matches how they feel about the word.

Words to use with the model:

Teacher	School	Mum	P. E.
Pets	Dad	Music	Friends
Classroom	Brother	Sister	Maths
Principal	Spelling	Recess time	Grandparents
Reading	Lunchtime	Bedroom	Holidays
Before school	Weekends	Computing	After school
Canteen	Support with learning	Snack time	Story time
Getting to school	Night-time	Homework	Fitness

Figure 13 How are you feeling today? model

Sentence Completion Test

Students complete answers to the questions. Questions can be adapted to meet the needs of a student. For example, a sheet could be for adolescent boys or adolescent girls specifically.

Name: _____ Sex: _____ Date of birth: _____

School: _____ Year: _____ Date: _____

1. I like _____
2. The happiest time _____
3. I want to know _____
4. At home _____
5. At night time _____
6. I am sorry for _____
7. The best _____
8. Boys _____
9. What upsets me _____
10. People _____
11. A mother _____
12. I feel _____
13. My greatest fear _____
14. In my previous school _____
15. I can't _____
16. Sports _____
17. When I was younger _____
18. My nerves _____
19. Other pupils _____
20. I suffer _____
21. I failed _____
22. Reading _____

23 My mind _____

24 The future _____

25 I need _____

26 Examinations are _____

27 I am best when _____

28 Sometimes _____

29 What annoys me _____

30 I hate _____

31 At school _____

32 I am very _____

33 The only trouble _____

34 I wish _____

35 My father _____

36 I secretly _____

37 Writing is _____

38 Dancing _____

39 My greatest worry is _____

40 Most girls _____

41 Facebook _____

42 The computer_____

Sample note-keeping page

Name of student: Date: Session number:

Notes:

Actions:

Follow-up:

References

Bailey, V., Baker, A-M., Cave, L., Fildes, J., Perrens, B., Plummer, J., and Wearring, A. (2016). Mission Australia's 2016 Youth Survey Report, Mission Australia.

Pikas, A. (2002). New Developments of the Shared Concern Method. *School Psychology International*, *23*, 307–31.

Index

absenteeism 17
academic attainment 18, 73
active listening 6, 16–17, 37, 38–9
adaptability 1
addiction to technology 73–5
advice, giving 13
advocacy 9
age of students 33–4
anger 9, 13, 23; counselling for 83–5; grief and 54, 55, 59, 60; as sign that counselling may be needed 20, 21; as symptom of depression 96
anxiety 3, 9, 73, 86–93
appearance 20
apps 93
artwork 19, 56
asking for help 14
attention seeking 21
Autism Spectrum Disorder (ASD) 17, 38, 68

background information 17, 22, 29, 32
baggage 14, 15
behaviour change 17
behavioural management 13, 21
being there for students 7, 10
bereavement 53, 55, 56; *see also* grief
Beyond Blue 93, 94
bias 11–12
Black Dog Institute 4, 94
blame 59, 60, 61
body image 86
body language 7–8, 13, 67; friendship cues 90; initial greetings 31–2; listening 16, 38; signs that counselling may be needed 17
bounce backs 62
boundaries 25–6
brainstorming 37, 41–2, 45
bullseye analysis 65–6, 67
bullying 76–82; breaking confidentiality 13; holding grudges 12; instances 41; Miracle Question 40; personal baggage 14
burn out 100

career guidance 69–72
Career Wedding Cake 71

caring 3, 7
change, identifying 39, 40
clarification 39
clarity, seeking 16
clichés 58
closed questions 38, 56
clothing 20
cognitive restructuring 47, 48, 49
communication 3, 11, 31
computer addiction 74
computer security 24
confidence 9, 19, 42–3
confidentiality 9, 25–8, 49; breaking 13, 26–8, 38; working with parents 50
control 47–8, 49, 91–2
coping skills 2
counselling: anger 83–5; anxiety 86–93; building the counselling relationship 32–3; bullying 76–82; career guidance 69–72; definition of 10; ending the counselling relationship 44–5; friendships 65–8; grief 52–64; older and younger students 33–4; setting 29–31; signs which suggest a need for 17–22; Solution-Focused Counselling Model 35–46, 84, 85, 99–100; techniques 47–51; technology addiction 73–5; what it is 6–10; what it is not 11–14
crying 17, 21–2, 57, 61, 87, 96
cues 17, 90

data security 24
deal with fact (DWF) 48, 49, 89–90, 91
decision-making 1
deep breathing 2
denial 59, 60
depression 4, 53, 61; counselling for 94–8; definition of 94; technology addiction 73
desensitisation 47, 48, 49
diagnosed conditions 17
discipline 12
disputes 6
disruptive behaviour 21
distractions 12
drama 19, 86

Egan, Gerard 7
embarrassment 31, 33, 85
empathy 7, 11, 13, 15–16, 38
empty chair technique 42–3, 47, 48, 49
ending the counselling relationship 44–5
enthusiasm for learning 5
exams 47, 48, 53, 86, 88–9, 91
exercise 62, 92, 97, 99
experience 3, 14
eye contact 7, 8, 17

family structure 101–3
family therapy 75
fatigue 73
fear 47, 54, 87, 88
feedback 3, 98
feelings: reflecting 16, 38; scaling 90–1
first impressions 29
First Sign 37, 43
flexibility 1
follow-up sessions 44, 45
free writing 92
friends 21, 62, 65–8; anxiety 86, 87–8, 90; depression 95; fear of making 49
friendship groups 21, 61, 67, 90

games 23
gaming 73, 74
genograms 101–3
giving 97, 99
goals 10, 97
Graceful Exit Line (GEL) 31, 67
grief 14, 18, 52–64
group work 57
grudges 12
gunship parents 5

happiness 97
health professionals 51, 92–3
Healthline 95
helicopter parents 5
help, asking for 14
home, avoiding going 17
homework challenges 48, 49
humour 2, 42

imagery 43, 47, 49
instances 37, 41

jigsaw puzzles 23, 29

'keeping yourself safe' 22, 24, 28, 29
kindness 3

lawn mower parents 5
leaning 8
learned helplessness 11
learning 5, 97, 99
learning difficulties 18–19

legal issues 24, 25, 26
life experience 3, 14
listening 6, 11, 12, 16–17, 36, 83; grief counselling 58, 64; Solution-Focused Counselling Model 37, 38–9
loss 52, 53

mediation 3, 6
medication 95
meltdowns 21, 22
Mental Health America 95
mental health conditions 4, 5
mental imagery 43, 47, 49
Method of Shared Concern (Pikas Method) 77, 82
mindfulness 99
Mindfulness App 93
Miracle Question 37, 39–40
Mission Australia study 4, 5, 31, 94
mobile phones 47, 49, 73
Mood Gym 93
moving forward after grief 59, 62
music 19, 32, 48, 56, 71, 86, 92

non-judgementalism 9, 38
notes 24–5, 106

open questions 38
opening lines 36, 37
openness 8
organisational skills 1

parents: breaking confidentiality 27; children's technology addiction 75; grief 55; helicopter 5; involvement of 22; listening 17; pressure from 14; social media and bullying 80; as source of information 21; talking to 32, 50–1
personal baggage 14, 15
physical education 19, 20
Pikas, Anatol 77, 82
Plan of Action 37, 42–3, 45
play times 84, 85
Positive Message 37, 44, 45
positive people 97, 99
positive self-talk 43, 47, 48, 88
positive thinking 62, 81, 88, 97
posters 23, 29
posture 8
power relations 11
preparation for life 4
problem-solving skills 1–2, 4–5, 6, 11
problems 35–6
professional agencies 51, 92–3
promises 36
prompting 8, 23, 34, 38
puppets 57

quick thinking 1

rapport 22, 23, 27, 31–2
realisation stage of grief 59, 61–2
record-keeping 24–5, 106
referral sources 10
reflecting feelings 16, 38
reinforcement 3
relationships: family 102; with professional agencies 51; teacher–student relationships 3, 85; *see also* friends
relaxing 8
representing students 9
resilience 4, 5, 40, 80–1
role modelling 2, 47, 49, 76, 85, 86
routines 56, 58, 62

safe places 7, 83, 84
scaling 90–1
Scaling Question 37, 40–1, 45, 96
school camps/excursions 20–1
school experience of counsellor 14
school yards 84, 85
self-care 51, 99–100
self-esteem 19, 73, 79, 80, 81, 97
self-harm 21–2, 26, 38, 94; *see also* suicidality
self-regulation 35
self-talk 43, 47, 48, 88
Sentence Completion Test 36, 104–5
separation 14
sexual activity 51
SFCM *see* Solution-Focused Counselling Model
shock 59–60
signs 17–22
silence 8, 38, 39, 56, 58
skills: anxiety 93; awareness of student's 11; follow-up sessions 44; grief counselling 63; homework challenges 48; practising your 98; social 68; teachers' skills 1–3; teaching of 2, 9
social media 21; anxiety 86; bullying 79–80; friendships 67–8; grief 54, 57

social skills 68
SOLER acronym 7–8
Solution-Focused Counselling Model (SFCM) 35–46, 84, 85, 99–100
speaking skills 9
sport 32, 33, 53, 71, 84; anxiety 86; bullying 76, 80; need for practice 48; routines 62; technology addiction 73
square posture 8
St Lukes 23
strengths and weaknesses 14–16
stress 4, 9, 50, 56, 96, 97, 99–100
study pressures 4
suicidality 26–7, 38, 97
summarising 39
support networks 50, 51, 55, 64, 90
sympathy 13

taking notice 97, 99
talk, helping students to 10, 16, 22–3, 38, 103
talking to students 6
teacher–student relationships 3, 85
teaching of skills 2, 9
technology addiction 73–5
teenagers 54, 56–7
thought blocking 47, 48, 88–9, 97
time, making 7
training 11, 98
trust 9, 13, 25

value-free stance 12
values 11, 12

warning signs 17–22
whiteboards 23–4, 25, 39, 49, 56, 88, 91
withdrawal 17, 54, 61, 73, 87, 94, 97
worry time 92
writing 19, 92

For Product Safety Concerns and Information please contact our EU
representative GPSR@taylorandfrancis.com
Taylor & Francis Verlag GmbH, Kaufingerstraße 24, 80331 München, Germany

www.ingramcontent.com/pod-product-compliance
Lightning Source LLC
Chambersburg PA
CBHW080940300426
44115CB00017B/2895